Praise For Books
By Dale Carlson

STOP THE PAIN: ADULT MEDITATIONS

"Carlson has drawn together the diverse elements of the mind, the psyche, and the spirit of science...Carlson demystifies meditation using the mirrors of insight and science to reflect what is illusive and beyond words."

— R.E. Mark Lee, Director,
  Krishnamurti Publications America

CONFESSIONS OF A BRAIN-IMPAIRED WRITER

Confessions of a Brain-Impaired Writer is "worth twice the price of admission. An uplifting, sassy, and entertaining read."

— *The Book Reader*

"Dale Carlson captures with ferocity the dilemmas experienced by people...*Confessions* is an important read."

— Dr. Kathleen Laundy, Psy.D., M.S.W.
  Yale School of Medicine

STOP THE PAIN: TEEN MEDITATIONS

"Dale Carlson invites [those] who are facing the problems of life to put their minds in harmony with all of the universe by sitting still, being quiet, and paying attention to everything in their lives...techniques to overcome fear, loneliness, anger, and depression.... Pictures by Carol Nicklaus are charming and illustrate the text accordingly."

— Louise Foerster, *Lorgnette, Heart of Texas*

STOP THE PAIN: TEEN MEDITATIONS

"Five hundred years ago Dale Carlson would have been the village elder who, in the quietness and wisdom of her life, would have helped you see beyond the veil of the known."

— R.E. Mark Lee, Director,
Krishnamurti Publications America

"If Dale Carlson can't get [someone] to pay attention, maybe there isn't a way. Her writing is easy, non-intrusive, packed with gentle...tips.... A lively, quiet book."

— *The Book Reader*

"Much good advice is contained in these pages."

— *School Library Journal*

GIRLS ARE EQUAL TOO: THE TEENAGE GIRL'S HOW-TO-SURVIVE BOOK (ALA Notable Book)

"Well-documented and written with intelligence, spunk and wit."

— *The New York Times Book Review*

"Spirited, chatty, and polemical, *Girls Are Equal Too* gives a crash course in gender discrimination; from the history of women's subordination to self-empowerment today."

— *Publishers Weekly*

"Clearly documented approach to cultural sexism in our society, Carlson reviews the image of women in the educational process, in the media, in dating and marriage."

— *School Library Journal*

WHERE'S YOUR HEAD?
PSYCHOLOGY FOR TEENAGERS
(Christopher Book Award)

"A practical focus on psychological survival skills... covers theories of human behavior, emotional development, mental illnesses and treatment."

— *Publishers Weekly*

"Thoughtful discussion of different theories of mental and emotional development, mental illnesses, and their treatment, and common problems and their causes."

— *The Science Teacher,* National Science Teachers Association

LIVING WITH DISABILITIES

"Excellent introductory handbooks about disabilities and special needs. They discuss medical conditions and rehabilitation, feelings and adaptive technology, and responsible attitudes both on the part of people with disabilities and people temporarily without them. The emphasis is on our common humanity, not our differences."

— Lynn McCrystal, M.ED., Vice-president, The Kennedy Center

WILDLIFE CARE FOR BIRDS AND MAMMALS

"Informative and to the point...ethical...wonderful job illustrating...I would recommend the series as a good introduction to rehabilitation...well-organized, quick to look through."

— Gail Buhl, wildlife biologist, *NWRA Quarterly*

STOP THE PAIN
Adult Meditations

STOP THE PAIN

Adult Meditations

Dale Carlson
Pictures By Carol Nicklaus

BICK PUBLISHING HOUSE   2000   MADISON, CT

Edited by Director Editorial Ann Maurer
Associate Editor Anna B. Smith
Book Design by Jennifer A. Payne
Cover Design by Greg Sammons

www.bickpubhouse.com

Library of Congress Cataloging-in-Publication Data

Carlson, Dale Bick.
    Stop the pain : adult meditations / Dale Carlson ; pictures by Carol Nicklaus.
        p.   cm.
    Includes bibliographical references (p.   ) and Index.
    ISBN 1-884158-21-8
    1. Meditations. 2. Conduct of life. I. Title.
BL624.2C36   2000
158. 1'2--dc21   99-40026
                                                            CIP

Distributed by BookWorld Services, Inc.
Whitfield Park Loop
Sarasota, FL 34243
or Fax 800/777-2525
or Fax 941/753-0396

Printed by McNaughton & Gunn, Inc., USA

In Dedication

To serious people everywhere who have inquired deeply, sometimes painfully, always honestly and with good will, into questions about their lives and all lives on earth. And to those questioners who continue to take part in meditation, in dialogue, in observing that right action in this new millennium cannot be based in the old, in the past, either in our personal lives or in community.

To the late J. Krishnamurti (1895-1986), who taught us all the necessity of being free of any psychological authority, to look critically at ourselves as the source of our own suffering, and to find the joy of going beyond the limits and prisons of those selves into freedom.

To R.E. Mark Lee, whose gentle wisdom and immaculate sensitivity informs matters of life as well as aesthetics.

And to Ray Fisher, friend and philosopher, who opened the door.

Acknowledgments

Special thanks to Virginia L. Rath, Ph.D., and Hannah B. Carlson, M.Ed., C.R.C., for their patient editing and for their expertise in their various fields of neuroscience, biology, psychology, and psychotherapy. Our thanks also to Ann Maurer for her editorial direction.

Gratitude always to Jennifer A. Payne for her gifted book design, and to Carol Nicklaus for her inspired pictures. And our thanks to Greg Sammons for his marvelous covers.

BOOKS BY DALE CARLSON

FICTION:
The Mountain of Truth
The Human Apes
Triple Boy
Baby Needs Shoes
Call Me Amanda
Charlie the Hero

NONFICTION:
Stop the Pain: Teen Meditations
Confessions of a Brain-Impaired Writer
Manners that Matter

with HANNAH CARLSON

NONFICTION:
Where's Your Head?: Psychology for Teenagers
Girls Are Equal Too: The Teenage Girl's How-to-Survive Book
Living with Disabilities
Basic Manuals for Friends of the Disabled:
    6 Volume Series

with IRENE RUTH

Wildlife Care for Birds and Mammals
First Aid for Wildlife

CONTENTS

Section Three
MAYHEM OR MEDITATION:
YOUR BRAIN CAN SAVE OR KILL YOU

Foreword

The world is our creation and we live in it, yet there is little that is original, which we can claim as creator. We repeat, copy, and imitate the ideas, symbols, and feelings of others from yesterday or a thousand years. Perhaps our lifelong self-fulfilling is our effort to become a true creator. Becoming something in life will distinguish me from everyone else and I will be appreciated, loved, and respected when at least one other person recognizes me as a true creator. This delusion holds the same fascination and has the same odds for success as any state lottery.

Stop the Pain: Adult Meditations documents and exposes the endlessly becoming in all of us. Adult problems and conflicts can be analyzed, written about, talked about, and laid bare in books, on television, and in the drama staged on the boards of our daily living. Yet, we are not really changed deeply, inwardly, with all this. Carlson has drawn together the diverse elements of the mind, the psyche, and the spirit of science to make the case that thought is an inadequate instrument to solve all problems; that psychological becoming is the root of conflict; that the problem in relationship, with money and work can change only when one has a meditative approach.

Meditation is beyond its own definition and its promise. There is a mystery in meditation that the ancients, practitioners, and authors of books on meditation find hard to describe. The nonqualifiable, non-physical world inside us is as vast as the outer reality that is beyond science. Meditation is a door into that vast universe. Carlson demystifies meditation using the mirrors of insight and science to reflect what is illusive and beyond words. Where there is meditation without a center as meditator then there is real meditation. This becomes a clear fact as the Carlson mirrors are used, set aside, and becoming ceases. The words, examples, suggestions on getting started, and quotes from the wise are simply to get you to look at your psychological thinking and see the havoc it creates, and then to stop inappropriate thinking. It is no more than just being silent and looking; these are the keys to that door of meditation.

R.E. Mark Lee, Director
Krishnamurti Foundation, America

Introduction

THE UNIVERSE IS BEAUTIFUL: SO WHY AM IN PAIN?

The Universe Is Beautiful:
So Why Am I In Pain?

Whenever we have a conversation with another human being who is physically close, we exchange molecules with every breath. I breathe in your air, you breathe in mine. My molecules enter your body, your molecules enter mine. We take each other in, literally, physically, as well as psychologically. Since I become part of you, and you become part of me every time we open our mouths, it is easy to see why the world does not need any more bad breath.

Since you can only breathe out whatever you are within, psychologically as well as physically, clearly you can bless or contaminate wherever you go. With nearly six billion people spinning together on this globe now, you are going to affect a lot of people. It is best, perhaps, to pay attention to what you are that you're giving off.

That is a dictionary definition of meditation: "to ponder over, to reflect on, to pay attention to."
That's all. But that's a great deal.

Meditation, the word 'meditation' and the vision of someone who 'meditates,' has exercised a fascination over me all of my adult life. Something incandescent, deeply mysterious, and certainly transformational, I thought, granted the meditator insight into self, god, the meaning of life in this universe, that pierced the confusion and despair that so often gripped me in my early adulthood. So whenever I came across someone, in a book or in a person, who seemed able to teach me the meaning of the magical word, I came to a halt and listened. In the sixties particularly, gurus swarmed the earth. With other 'seekers of truth' I chanted, I did zazen, I focused on candles and mantras. I read Christian, Hindu, Muslim, Native American, Jewish, Buddhist scripture. Everywhere people talked about insight and awareness and meditation. It felt righteous to sit up all night, with the civil rights and women's rights movements and anti-war demonstrations for background, kicking over the traces of traditional scripture and liturgy, making all these new sounds and staring at lighted candles instead.

Nothing, however, changed or altered the fact that we were all suffering and had no idea who to blame or who was in charge of fixing everything. Psychotherapy suggested candidates, but its explanations neither alleviated everybody's suffering nor explained why blaming didn't seem to lighten the load.

A philosopher friend handed me something to read, someone to read, who said, or seemed to say:

"If you will stop making messes, there won't be any. And the way to do this isn't chants and rituals and long chats. The way to do this is to pay attention to what you are doing, thinking, saying, in the first place.

"It's you who are the problem, you with your automatic agendas and knee-jerk reactions. Stop. Look with new eyes. Understand this, and you have the solution."

I have been unable to react with automatic unconcern since. Thank god. I hope someone's mind, someone's words, in the pages of this book will bring light to you as that teacher's words brought light to me, and help you to find your way to stop your pain.

The second most interesting fact I have discovered about meditation, aside from that it is not an instant magic ritual fix, is that the quiet of meditation produces such a variety of states of mind. Insights do occur. But not punctually. Sometimes meditative states produce the grocery list.

For me, meditation was never a trivial pursuit. To see into human nature was my goal, beginning with my own. To find out why our natures suffer so deeply, so painfully. To find the way to stop it instead of just using pleasure to escape it temporarily. To stop hurting and being hurt by other human beings who ought to be my comrades, not strangers peering out of other armored tanks just like mine.

The constant attention to daily living I call meditation has made a difference in these more than twenty years since the grueling anguish of my late thirties. Pharmacology has helped. Neurobiology has helped. But voices like those in this book, reading and dialogue, group and private, psychological and physical forms of meditation among many teachers and students, have transformed my understanding of everything that happens to me, to all of us. One criticism of this book by a scientist friend is that I speak with authority but have established no authority for what I speak. I was delighted to hear it. We are each our own authority in meditation. You sit. You listen. That is all.

So I began to learn, and went on learning. Meditation does not mean standing on your head in a corner of the room making peculiar sounds in strange tongues. The moving practices like hatha yoga, walking, martial arts, or the sitting practices like focusing on a candle, counting inhalations and exhalations, chanting, mantra, and all the rest, are excellent preparation in quieting the body, oxygenating the brain and the nervous system. But these are done so that meditation, attention, can take place in the quiet, the stillness that follows, when your thoughts, feelings, questions can be pondered over and insight can take place in the gaps between thoughts.

That this head-standing, candle-lighting, incantation-saying, and breath-counting isn't really the point, should be a relief.

Meditation itself is actually both simpler and more difficult.

True meditation is a constant, or as nearly constant as you can manage, attention in your daily life. And it is a lot harder to pay attention to what you are doing, thinking, feeling, saying; how you are reacting, behaving; how you are breathing, sitting, working, making love, parenting, playing basketball, cards, or with the bowling league, the PTA, your friends and family and coworkers — than it is to stand on your head. What we need to attend to, what is most important, is whether we are giving pain to ourselves and everyone else, or kindness.

Life is a shock. No one prepares us for this. At home we are taught the value of making a living; at school we are taught skills in making that living. In few places are we taught skills in living itself.

So we rocket between the glorious joys of sunsets, music, falling in love, the birth of a child — and the chronic anxiety of never feeling comfortable in our own skins. We experience moments of appalling pain from which there seems no escape. The screens of our own minds showing in reruns the hurts of our own lives; the television and movie screens run and rerun the horror shows of other people's lives all over the world. Life shocks with the suffering from fear, loneliness, from anger and despair. It stuns from being poor, or emotionally ill, from physical disability, from being afraid to die. It hurts from violence, whether in the street from crime, or at home with family, or in competition at work. It hurts from failing, or being afraid to fail, on the job, in relationships. Depression, self-hate, rejection, envy, feeling different, left out, having to try too hard to keep up — the causes of suffering, of shame and pain and sheer terror come and go with every breath.

Life also hurts just from lack of caring. How deeply do we care about the birth of one more deformed baby, the murder of 800,000 Tutsis, people devastated by another catastrophic flood in Bangladesh — how much do they care about trouble among us? And that these moments of appalling pain, appalling, are so shot through with beauty, the sunset as dazzling over the swollen bellies of starving children as on the snow peaks of the Himalayan mountains, leaves the human system in a constant state of bewilderment — if it is aware enough to notice.

Along with the brutality and the beauty is the insistent irony of loneliness.

How is it everyone, I mean everyone, is so lonesome on a planet that rumbles, roils, screams, and sweats with so many billions of people?

It is a blow to human pride that we have failed to answer our own main questions, the questions people have always asked, the questions that drive us into meditation:

1. Why are we here?

2. Who's in charge?

3. Why life hurts, angers, bores us so much of the time?

4. What we are supposed to do about it?

5. If nothing, if only to bear it, is there a point to all this pain?

6. If the universe (God, Brahmin, Allah, Great Spirit, Buddha, Tao) is benign, how come there are babies being maimed?

7. If the universe is malign, why don't we all just kill ourselves now and have done with it?

8. Is it possible to change ourselves so we feel and cause less pain?

9. Can one human being make a difference?

Some other questions that have always provoked meditation:

1. Are we alone in this universe, on this rock rattling through space? Spooky, the consequences of that. Equally spooky are the consequences of not being alone. Either contemplation drives people to totter on the edge of madness.

2. Why is my brain trying to drive me insane with its crazy thoughts? Going too many rounds with this one will drive you over the edge.

3. Is my very self the mind-altering chemical that sets off so much bizarre neuronal circuitry?

The trouble, of course, is not what thoughts you are thinking, but with the process of thought itself. Understanding the processes of your thoughts is meditation itself — and the subject of this book.

Another trouble that must be pointed out is that most of us are never taught to expect pain from our own brains. We don't know where the pain is, where it comes from, and what to do about it. We are never taught that it isn't so much life, but our brains' reactions to life that causes the ache. It's the baggage our brains have been stuffed with that mostly causes all the pain — what we're taught we are, what we're taught to want, what we're taught to hate and fear — and then our brains come up with solutions that cause even more pain. If yours isn't going to kill you, you will have to pay attention to what it is doing, and how it is reacting to everything. And learn how to offload, delete, dump some of its weight. Or learn at least to rewire its habits of thinking, its habitual neuronal circuitry.

Again, this is what meditation is, what the word means: to pay attention. As I was taught early on:

- Stop what you're doing

- Sit down

- Be quiet

- And pay attention

What most of us do when our brains hurt, when we have mental pain, is try to fix the pain by escaping it: in alcohol or drugs, sex, food, spending or gambling money, in exhausting obsessions with a lover, with the need for approval, with work, the status of position or possessions, compulsive television watching and other fantasies — anything that will take the edge off.

The difficulty is that now we're stuck with two problems: with the original pain (not dealt with, so still there); and with the results of whatever was used as an escape (you're fat, you're addicted to something or someone, you're broke) as well. Again, it's a big shock how much life can hurt. But it's a bigger shock that we never got taught, along with reading, writing, how to turn on a stove or off a computer, how to deal with emotional pain.

And this is true whether we live in the projects or on Park Avenue, in the suburbs or the inner city, whether we are male or female, Latino, African American, European American, from India, China, or an island in the Pacific Ocean. Personal and cultural differences are superficial. The whole human race belongs to the same species, with the same *a priori* spatial perceptions, the same biological agenda (we all need to breathe, eat, defecate, reproduce), the same emotions (fear, anger, joy, affection, passion). We are as alike as ants. Everyone in the human race, give or take a talent or gender or a disordered gene, has the same brain.

So far, we only seem to use about 15% of our brains. This is encouraging, when you think about it. Imagine if we could learn to use the other 85%, and use it better. And what we know about the brain still isn't much. We still don't know how the brain's neural connections create either self or self-consciousness. We still don't know why our species is technologically ingenious enough to gather dust from Mars and yet continues to point bombs and nerve gas at its own kind.

It seems, according to some specialists in neuroscience and human consciousness, that the human brain took a wrong turn in its developmental evolution. It *thought* it saw solid bodies instead of a universe full of atoms all in relationship to each other. It *invented* separate and different selves for those bodies instead of correctly seeing connected, nearly identical selves. This was the beginning of loneliness and fear and competition and killing, this mistake. This mistake, the big one, is that we have mistaken the enemy — it is not each other but our own brains telling us we are not each other.

We need to correct this mistake, understand that society isn't them, it's all of us. Since we all have the same brain, and every brain affects other brains, if even one of us changes, learns to understand and do away with mental suffering and the grief, hurt, and fear that make for anger and violence, that change will affect all brains, all society, the minds of all of us. This is a staggering realization: it overrides that program that sometimes insinuates itself into our darkest hours. You know, the one that says, "Life sucks. Then you die."

It becomes more and more clear, then, the more you look at it. Meditation is paying attention to what is going on in your brain, not running away from it. It does not take an outside specialist or expert. Anyone can see that our brains have two main capacities. Our brains have thought, which is the reaction of memory, all the accumulated stuff of experience, learned and stored knowledge; and we have the capacity for immediate, fresh observation of what's going on. You can see by watching your own brain, we are either thinking in terms of past reactions, or we are observing with fresh insight. Meditation is not a trance induced by your self or someone else. Meditation is simply an awareness of these two capacities and how they work. It is paying attention to your reactions, what you like, what you don't like, the food, the culture, the habits of daily life and thought, your attitudes about people, religion, country, family, everything you were brought up to. The point is to see all of this information — not just obey it all blindly. See what is actually going on inside and outside of you, not what you'd like yourself and the world to be, but actually what it is. The point is to transform our selves, so our behavior isn't based on past fear and anger, but on something else entirely. And to the extent you change the ways of your self, you change everyone around you. All consciousness affects all of us. Thought is actually a material process.

Obviously, both physical and mental pain happen. Somebody we love will die. We or our children will fail, be rejected, feel lonely, left out. We will fear death, age, sickness, feel pity for our own life or the poor and sick of the world. It is thought's fear of pain and its effects on the very self thought has invented, that turns pain into long-term suffering. And mental suffering, according to the new neurobiologists, is as physically based as any cracked elbow. But there's a way to handle emotional pain so that it passes instead of causing further damage. Analysis, your own, a friend's, or a professional analyst's, may comfort, but it rarely brings relief. Intellectual explanations seldom work in permanently dissolving psychological problems: usually, you're left with both the explanations and the pain. Use your brain, but use it in a different way. Instead of thought and analysis which sometimes prolong and often confuse, we'll go into the use of insight, awareness of the brain's processes, to get over emotional pain far more quickly.

So even if you're numbing or escaping your fears or anxieties, resentments or rages, in all the usual ways, here's a different way to stop the pain, either now or later on. In this new millennium, change the atoms and molecules, the circuitry of the mind with meditation instead.

The point is:

- Pain happens: you can learn not to suffer over it.

- Relief from psychological pain, mental and emotional suffering, comes with *paying attention* to what you are doing — not trying to *fix it* with some technique long after it happens, nor from debilitating escapes.

- Oddly, it is this very attention — a deep attention, not a superficial glance — that transforms the pain, dissolves it, evaporates it.

- This attention is a way of life, a daily attention, not just a psychological Band-Aid when the going gets rough.

M editation is simply the discovery, for yourself, of the inner workings of the self, your self as you discover it on your own — not according to therapists, shamans, politicians, as if we were in a perpetual childhood and expected to turn our selves over to the care of some adult. This book is about everyone's ability to meditate. We all (not just priests, rabbis, mullahs, ministers, nuns, and not just the Hindus, the Christians, the Jews, Muslims, Native Americans, and Buddhists) have this means to understand what we are, to keep what we want in ourselves, and to change the rest.

This book is probably best read slowly, a little at a time, pausing often to try out what you are reading. Because what you are reading is not the book's words, but the book of yourself. And understanding yourself is not done once and for all. It is done constantly, every reaction as it happens, everything you do and say, every day. People who don't know themselves can be dangerous, or at the very least insensitive. People who do know themselves, know enough to be careful and remember that the rules of living begin with: first, do no harm.

Here's how meditation works.

Section One

TO WAKE, OR TO
GO ON SLEEPING

CHAPTER ONE
The Big Question: What Do We Really Want Out Of Our Lives?

If what we want is to be happy, the human race has a strange way of going about it. It's our brains. On important issues, our brains either give us conflicting information, very little, or none at all. Why is that? We've had these brains a long time as a species, four million years or so, say some scientists. So why won't they work properly to give us what we want?

All most people want is to feel good, to escape pain. We want some inner peace; we want those judgmental voices inside our heads to shut up once in a while. We want enough security so we can sleep nights. We want enough success to prove we have a right to take up space in our society. We want to belong, to have lasting and loving relationships, with a mate, with family, friends, coworkers, community. We want enough money to pay the bills, perhaps enough left over for fun now and senility later on. Most people want some pleasure, many want beauty, some want immortality, or at least to skip death.

What goes wrong? It seems, no matter what we do to escape, our brains are more suited to suffering than any other activity. We seem to be wired, not for peace, but for chaos. Memory, on which thought is based, is full of fear, anxiety, mourning for the past or terror of its recurrence. If the past seems bad, we are afraid it will come again with its pain. If the past seems good, the present, by comparison, must be painful. Our brains have formed extremely uncomfortable habits.

The brain records all experience; we carry with us all our pleasures and fears. Both are dangerous: the feared thing can happen again; the pleasure may be taken away. The real treasure in the brain is not pleasures with their attendant fears. The real treasure in our brains is the capacity for joy. To get at this capacity, we must shut thought, with its pleasures and fears, up. The brain is perfectly capable of rewiring itself to do this. We need technological thought, of course, or we couldn't speak languages, drive cars, know our own caves from the neighbors'. It's psychological thought that causes the glitch that prevents the happiness we seek, that causes that nagging undertow of agitation.

You've noticed some anomalies in your life by now, of course. The brass ring, for instance. Oddly hollow. You get the promotion, the dress, the award, the man you want or the woman, and ten minutes or a week later, you're still standing somewhere by yourself feeling as empty as you were before. You wonder again what's wrong with you that nothing fills you up, makes you feel happy, makes you feel finally safe. Insanity suggests itself, and not for the first time. The brain objects strenuously to living with suffering, struggling, loneliness, the feeling of purposelessness. It is at this point that people give up, turn on or turn off, drop out, run away. Escapes may temporarily stop the pain, but you've discovered cutting off doesn't help, that the solution is to connect. It's the secret of life, connection; to the universe, to nature, to community, to another person, to one's own life.

If we look at our brains, we discover that the very things we say we want, we inhibit. We want connection; but we hang onto the separate self that makes us lonely. We want sense; we behave in ways that bring us chaos. We want to be happy; but we suffer. We want security; but we're mostly in a panic. We want eternity; yet we're stuck with death.

Why can't we get where we're going?

If you're reading this book, you've already discovered the old solutions don't work, and it's time to try something different. Simple intelligence says, if you've tried north, east, and west, and come up with nothing, go south. And if your motor is trying to run your body off the road, is giving you too bumpy a ride, or has brought you to a stop, look under the hood at the engine.

If you discover that your brain, like everyone else's brain, is trying to kill you, either with pain or the ways it invents of escaping, with overwork or underwork in this society where it is so difficult to make a sane and intelligent livelihood, to raise and educate sane and intelligent children, to maintain loving and lasting relationships, that offers such accessible forms of mental suicide as just *your own conditioning suggests,* never mind drugs and television — have a look at it.

Watch your brain and its thoughts and ways, its habits, images, prejudices, desires, fears, its angers and anxieties, what bores it, upsets it, and the troubles these cause. Watch also what delights, brings joy. It is this watchful attention in daily life that is true meditation. And it is meditation itself that will change the way you feel, show you the right way to go whenever during your day or during your life an adjustment is required. Meditation is to look at everything inside you and out in the world with *new eyes*, a fresh perspective.

Before you say, what does it matter, with the bombings and the genocide, rape, and other horrifying brutalities, floods, starvation, and earthquakes taking place, with the racism, crime, random shootings, and computer viruses threatening us, the decimation of the earth's wildlife, think about the following things.

Five times before on our planet, life forms have become extinct, and come back, according to a group of cheerful scientists interviewed by Ted Koppel during a *Nightline* documentary. Asteroids hit the planet, the climate changes.

But life is still here. Life itself seems to be unquenchable. A cosmologist name Drake has worked out an equation that of the 200 billion stars in our galaxy, there are 100,000 planets on which life might occur. An energy source and liquid water created life here over four billion years ago — organic molecules from 3.85

billion years ago have been found here and on Mars, so perhaps anywhere in the universe there is light and liquid water — life! Easy. And it can get along fine, regenerate over and over again — with us or without us.

Flight, we are told, has evolved three separate times.

Why not intelligence? Even if we do blow ourselves up, the event will be nothing so special in the history of generations, and intelligence will probably evolve again as usual. Maybe next time in the form of a bird. Or from elsewhere in the galaxy from another planet, there will arrive an intelligent life form, mobile, with depth perception, the ability to communicate, with senses and reproductive organs. Because extraterrestrial life is not conveniently located, doesn't mean it isn't there.

But we're not done on this earth till the sun burns out, and by then we may even have discovered how to move on. It's life that matters, not just my life or yours, our generation or the next. So there's no excuse to give up. It's all just too glorious a spectacle.

People have always asked the same questions, of course:

- Is there a point of life?
- If so, what is it?
- What is the meaning of me?
- Is there a purpose for me?
- How do I find out? Whom do I ask?
- Is there God, or something watching over me? If there's God, and if God is good, how come there is all this suffering — conflict inside myself; argument, crime, war, disease outside?

My tremendous respect for the pain of human beings is how much we are willing to bear, how ongoing is our search for the truth of things, for an understanding of ourselves, of our world.

We go wrong, and we go stupid much too often, but we don't seem to give up. Pain makes us weary and we glaze over, bury deep, stay too busy to consider what we do. Still, some of us push on. As Annie Dillard once said, pain is a terrible thing to waste.

We can't just go on singing that old song all our lives, the one that begins "Why was I born, why am I living?" It's time to find out what we want and what we're doing here.

We want love and belonging and approval.

We want physical and emotional security.

We want permanence, even after death, immortality for our precious selves if possible, or at least membership in the Hall of Fame.

We want someone to tell us how to get these things.

We want to be happy, or at least less depressed and anxious. We wish we knew how.

The fact is, it is entirely possible to end fear and loneliness, the inner sadness and confusion that never seem entirely to go away. Each of us can find out what's running around inside our brains making us crazy and stop it.

Just not in the way we've been taught.

— • —

What is the good of my asking if there is happiness when I am suffering? Can I understand suffering? That is my problem, not how to be happy. I am happy when I am not suffering.

J. Krishnamurti
The Book of Life
Edited by R.E. Mark Lee

— • —

— • —

There is a difference between happiness and gratification. Perhaps you can find gratification but surely you cannot find happiness...it is a by-product of something else....

Study yourself, because what we are the world is. If we are petty, jealous, vain, greedy — that is what we create about us, that is the society in which we live.

J. Krishnamurti
The First and Last Freedom

— • —

Your mind creates your universe.

Richard Alpert (Ram Dass)
Journey of Awakening:
A Meditator's Guidebook

— • —

You are the light of the world.

Jesus of Nazareth
Holy Bible, Matthew 5:14

— • —

One of us may think in Mongol and another in Texan, but give or take a few such superficialities, all brains and the contents of their human consciousness are pretty much the same. This means that understanding your own brain for better and worse, allows you to understand everyone else as well. A good tool to help us all link arms and survive.

Since everything and everyone in the universe, all atoms everywhere, impact everything and everyone else, everything we do matters and we are all equally important in how we affect our common destiny.

— • —

All things are connected. Whatever befalls the earth, befalls the children of the earth.

Chief Seattle
Speech, 1853

— • —

CHAPTER TWO
Behind Bars:
Psychological Prison

A s you've been reading, you have begun to watch your thoughts, both the kinds of thoughts your brain entertains (must-do lists, opinions, likes, dislikes, controlling, possessive thoughts, desires, fears), and the way thoughts jump from one thing to another like monkeys in a cage. Some thoughts and thinking are technological, necessary to living one's life (the way to the bank or work, how to turn on lights, the computer, your name, in this day and age, your mother's maiden name). What we intend to discuss is psychological thought, the kind that ranges from irrelevant to downright dangerous. Which is why it is necessary to watch it.

This is very difficult, this watching of psychological thought. The watching must not be appalled, it must not be judgmental, it must not interfere. It must be only curious, certainly fearless, and without the conflicting views of judge, jury, and trial lawyers that inhabit all our brains.

The trouble with thought is that is interferes with clarity:

- Thought is paranoid: it is forever judging and commenting on what it is thinking.

- More than two-thirds of our thoughts are the same ones we had yesterday — not much new going on in there.

- Thought thinks that's all there is: it is unaware that it is unaware, that there is more than itself going on in the brain.

This is all because thought is the response of memory. Happily, whether thought knows it or not, the brain has two capacities. Thought is not all there is in the brain. There is also insight into, watching, observing thought inside and life outside the brain. But thought itself is, as we've seen, as you can continue to see by watching it, simply the response of memory, lots of memories, knowledge, the past, what was learned a long time ago, what was learned five minutes ago. Thought is not only conditioned; it continues to be conditionable.

As many of us have discovered, the secret of sorrow is loneliness, and the secret of a joyful life is connection, to other lives, to the universe, to our own lives. The trouble is, there is something in the way of connection. There's something that causes static, noise, interference with the connection. Peering closely at the thing that causes the interference, that is in fact the interference itself — it is the self invented by our very own thoughts.

The very commodity, the very jewel we are trying so hard to protect, is the very trouble, the very source of the chaos, the confusions, the conflict and violence, the loneliness we are trying so hard to escape. We hug to ourselves the very monster that is eating us alive and defending itself against anyone else who comes too close. As the entire job of the self is to protect itself, to live self-absorbed in self-interest, it's no wonder we sometimes have the feeling of living in loneliness, defensively, and behind bars, that we make literal and figurative war. And yet we go on celebrating this self. A major Western psychological tradition, full-blown in some psychotherapy circles, many religions, some philosophies, and in too many group therapies and workshops, is a dedication to self-esteem, self-respect, self-conceptualization, self-fulfillment.

— • —

We bring flowers to the very idol of our own destruction!

Ray Fisher
Unpublished Dialogues

— • —

We are a psychologically oddly constructed species. Seeing this is the most sensitive of meditations.

It is thought, as part of its response to memory, that invents what we call our SELF. Thought does this to give us a sense of security, of definition, of continuity, so we have the feeling we're not falling apart all the time, splitting into fragments, splinters, slivers of glass, that we're not temporal like other earthly objects.

We want a soul, a *me*, something that goes on and on. Thought invents the *me*, the self, to give us the sensation of permanence. We think permanence is the same as mattering.

Also, because the job of the brain is to protect the organism, to keep it alive, it makes and remembers images. Humans have no fur, claws, speed, or flight, to fight off other animals or escape them. We have our clever and cunning faculty for thought. Thought creates images, and helps us remember not to hang around lions. The trouble is, *thought is always creating images, remembering them, adding those images onto the original image of the SELF. And not just images of actual trouble like the lion, but psychological, holographic images that cause trouble, like racism, nationalism, sectarianism (I'm one thing, you're another). And we don't just have one self, we have lots of selves, actually. All those voices in our heads that keep arguing with each other, are all the different selves from all the different stages of our lives we've collected over the years. Sad to say, we add to them to give the brain a sense of there being always someone home guarding the bridge over the moat to the castle keep.* Then the collective SELF, while it thinks it is keeping you safe, becomes a prison from which it is hard to escape.

— • —

The intelligent man [or woman] who is proud of that intelligence
is like the condemned man who is proud of his large cell.

Simone Weil
Simone Weil: A Life

— • —

The SELF, with all its species/racial, cultural, gender, personal agenda memories, both conscious (open) and subconscious (hidden), becomes a house you live in behind locked doors. What you see through its windows is colored by all the information, prejudices, opinions, fears, pride, antagonism you've been handed down for a couple of million years. Thought is the warehouse full of baggage you've been handed. But it shuts you in as well as keeping others out.

As we have said, thought has its necessary place, or you couldn't read this book or find your car keys, make science or medicine or music, or even find the front door that closes your cave against the predators of the night.

But always remember, the brain does two things. It can think — and it can observe rightly, understand. Thought (old stuff) and intelligence (right-now understanding, observation) are separate functions. Thought, often called intellect, makes science —intelligence tells you what is the right or wrong thing to do with it. Thought, intellect, is good for the technical part of life, but intelligence only will tell you about the right actions to take. The dumb person is not the one who doesn't know the contents of books, but the one who doesn't understand the ways of herself or himself, doesn't understand the proper place of thought, and therefore gives and gets pain.

Meditation is the discovery of the area of the mind that *isn't* thought — that isn't the past, opinion, or knowledge. The area of the mind that *is* attention to what is going on *right now*. Meditation is the intelligence that takes no position.

Alex Comfort describes nonpositional intelligence in his book on physics, mind, and science in the twenty-first century. "In 1781 Immanuel Kant pointed out that time and space are not phenomena or things, but are simply ways of organizing data... Kant gave to what we now call 4-space (three linear dimensions and time) the title *a priori* — an invincible way of seeing with which human beings are born." Comfort adds to Kant's *a priori*'s, a fifth one, our other difficult human prejudice, 'positional identity' — the belief that there is an 'I' just inside or behind our heads that is separate from what we are observing. Comfort's study is called *demonics*, thinking of other ways in which thinking might take place, demon being shorthand for an intelligence which does not process information about the universe purely within the limitations of human terms, that understands in terms of physics/mathematics, other models or paradigms in other *a priori* modes. One such unlimited demon he calls Gezumpstein.

— • —

Gezumpstein is a universal or fundamental demon; that is to say,
he has no a prioris and his vision is inclusive and nonpositional.
Alex Comfort, M.D., D.Sc.
Reality and Empathy

— • —

It seems to me that Gezumpstein is the unfettered, unconditioned, nonpositional way to look, and that clear insight in the instant comes from no position except for freedom from position entirely. I personally find it infinitely satisfying when physics and metaphysics meet, when science and religion find the same truth.

What is going on in the instant, right now, changes all the time, like the river that flows on. You can't catch it and store it up, like knowledge. You just have to stay aware, awake all the moments of your life as it flows on. As we said in an earlier book, *Where's Your Head?*, "Understanding comes only through self-knowledge, which is awareness of one's total psychological process. Education, in the true sense, is this understanding of the ways of oneself and everyone else, not just information in books."

Leaving the cozy room you've created out of your thoughts can be terrifying — try changing your mind about anything, or try changing a single habit or addiction and you'll see how hard leaving anything familiar can be. And it won't work simply to redecorate, change the pictures on the walls or the furniture, or exchange one old habit for another. You have to make a dash out

the door into the sunlight to feel the difference between prison and freedom.

Prison is our old thoughts, and the accepted thoughts of society (really, the same thing, whether it's your parents' society, or your own peer society).

Escape now. Don't go on being used to habitual mental behavior. This doesn't mean running traffic lights or not paying taxes because you don't like what the government is doing in Yugoslavia or Iraq or Africa. There's no more freedom in real jail than mental jail. Freedom means paying attention to your psychological attitudes. Are they really yours? Are you stuck in them, trapped by ideas and behaviors you think you can't challenge? Or don't dare challenge?

— • —

We are used to thinking as a good thing, as that which makes us human. It can be quite a revelation to discover that so much of our thinking appears to be boring, repetitive, and pointless while keeping us isolated and cut off from the feelings of connection that we most value.

Mark Epstein, M.D.
Going to Pieces Without Falling
Apart: Lessons from Meditation
and Psychotherapy

— • —

CHAPTER THREE
Who And What Is Alive
In Your Brain?

Have you ever stared into your own eyes, say while you were brushing your teeth, and wondered if anybody or anything was in there, and if so, who? Or what?

The center of our thinking is ourselves. You can see this for yourself, by attending to your own thinking. We are peripherally aware of the birds, or the weather, someone across the room or in the next office, but mostly we are aware of anything peripheral in relationship to the 'me' — what I like, what I don't like, how this or that affects 'me.'

Considering how much time our 'selfs' take up, it might be interesting to ask, "Who and what am I?"

Have you ever counted all the different voices in your brain that whisper and nag and criticize you all day, every day, year in and year out? Have you ever wanted to tell your brain just for five minutes to be quiet and leave you in peace?

Those voices are simply our different selves. Some are conscious and we are aware of them. Some selves are hidden; they speak to us from the unconscious part of our brains, either the parts we don't want to remember and have repressed, or the parts so ancient we can't dredge them up into consciousness, such as the directions for breathing, moving muscles, digesting food. The structure of the personality, its problems, its arguments with itself, is not something we invent spontaneously from moment to moment. It is based on everything that has been downloaded into the brain.

You can examine your own personality in light of the following agendas, some software, some hardwired into all human brains. After all, meditation is only seeing the truth directly, not through someone else's view or according to this or any other book. Someone else's understanding of you isn't any more satisfying than watching someone else eat dinner when you're hungry. Begin by seeing all the agendas that make up all those voices that are all your selves.

- Animal, biological inheritance (we all have the basic urges for sex and aggression, the need to eat, eliminate, breathe, take shelter, stay alive).

- Cultural inheritance (this includes differing sexual behaviors, gender, color, religious politics, family and social habits, prejudices and preferences from table manners to carnal embrace).

- Personal experience (the physical, psychological development of your own particular life).

These are the agendas that create the selves, the voices, the din of' thou shalt' and 'thou shalt not' in our inner ears. It becomes increasingly clear that we don't have ONE self, we have dozens. What we call ego or self is just a lot of tape-recorded announcements jumbled together on a track. Actually, this item we call *myself* is a trick the brain plays, a group leader it invents to represent all the conscious parts of the brain that are aware of what's going on around us and regulate input and output.

Neurobiologists, molecular psychologists, biochemists, geneticists, neuroscientists, cognitive scientists, all sorts of brain specialists have discovered that information is scattered all throughout the brain: *there is no little homunculus, no little person, no single 'I' in there who makes decisions.* It just feels that way. But it's a group effort, really, that the brain makes, and our brain, in our civilization, has invented the notion of 'I.' The sad part of this is, it makes us feel separate from other 'I's' and is the cause of loneliness. We

are particularly insistent on this in the Western cultures, this 'I' am separate from you. We are willing to endure anguishes of appalling loneliness rather than acknowledge human beings are an ant colony or a beach of sand or an ocean of drops or accretions of molecules like everything else in the cosmos. In the East, Buddha's teaching is more widely respected, that the self is a just a myth and the source of all our troubles, that we are all part of a Great Self. In the West, we have inherited the Judeo-Christian cultural agenda, and we are adamant about having separate souls, separate selves.

That human cultures have not always encouraged this idea of 'I,' either pro or con, and originally more truly taught their children people are not separate identities, that the self is an inherited, communal affair, is clearly evident in the few primitive peoples who survive in Australia and Indonesia and South America where so-called civilization has only begun to erode these cultures. This neatly eliminates murder and war, as the children grow up knowing that if we kill someone else, we are killing part of ourselves and our communal futures. In point of fact, I'm not just my brother's keeper, I am my brother.

In both Western and Eastern cultures, great philosophers and scientists now understand that this *myself*, both personally and culturally, we all keep going on about is not a fact, but an invention of the brain's intellect, that we are scientifically not separate but interconnected. Separate names and labels are words for convenience of discussion; they imply different biological structures (after all structure is the way life fights entropy, predators, and parasites as cognitive scientist Stephen Pinker points out in his *How the Mind Works*). But labels exist for convenience; they do not imply a difference in essence, the basic building blocks of atoms and molecules.

That while we each evolve our own envelope of skin to keep our insides from falling out and the rain from getting in makes us appear separate to the naked eye, we are about as differentiated as raindrops, is proposed by many leading minds.

The biochemist Rupert Sheldrake proposed, and proved in animal experiments, that new behavior learned by one or a few members of a species is then learned quickly by the entire species, that there are causation fields, akin to magnetic fields, aside from DNA, to explain everybody's and everything's behavior, so that what occurs to a single member of a species does not remain individual and private, but directly affects all other members. He postulates a far more collective memory affects our behavior than any individual consciousness.

— • —

The morphogenetic fields of all past systems become present to any subsequent similar system...For example, the molecules of a complex organic chemical crystallize in a characteristic pattern...a plant takes up the form characteristic of its species because past members of the species took up that form...as an animal acts instinctively in a particular manner because similar animals behaved like that previously.

Rupert Sheldrake
A New Science of Life

— • —

We could have listened to the English philosopher John Locke three hundred years ago when he said labels do not make something so:

— • —

Genera and species...depend on collections of ideas man has made, and not on the real nature of things...Our distinct species are nothing but distinct complex ideas, with names annexed to them.

John Locke
Essay on Human Understanding

— • —

Today, Daniel Dennett, cognitive scientist, writes to the point that thought alone, not fact, creates the illusion of a separate self:

— • —

The trouble with brains, it seems, is that when you look in them, you discover that there's nobody home. No part of the brain is the thinker that does the thinking or the feeler that does the feeling.

Daniel C. Dennett
Consciousness Explained

— • —

B ut you don't have to take anyone's word for this fact, that 'you' are just a bit of fiction in the story you're inventing about your life. Haven't you ever looked in your eyes, as we've asked earlier, while you were staring into them over a toothbrush, and had the feeling there's nobody home? Haven't you ever said to yourself, "I have to pull myself together?" because when you're alone and drifting there's that feeling, comfortable or nervous, that you're all separate pieces, not a cohesive, singular person after all?

You're right on both counts. Your body is as contained in its own feathers as any starling in a flock (not much different, one starling from another, but breathing on its own). But the 'you' of you is *not* an actual entity; and there *isn't* anyone home.

This fact explains two sensations we all experience.

1. The sensation of getting lost in a movie, or music, a game, or a book, lost in the sight of the sun setting over the mountains or the sea, in the eyes of someone with whom you've fallen in love.

   There's no *me*, no *self* then, is there? Until 'you' come back and run around inside your head collecting the fragments that, put together, constitute the *you*.

2. The sensation of the hole inside us every one of us keeps trying to fill. That empty hole at the core of us into which we stuff possessions and status, food, sex, drugs, ambition, a frantic busyness, as if one more car, romance, drink, lottery ticket, the right clothes, job, mate, or child will finally do the trick and fill us up. Some people keep machinery, electronic and otherwise, running; some like myself keep the mouth running to drown out the emptiness. Some people try a new church, temple, guru, shaman, psychic. Some people go into psychotherapy complaining of feeling empty. Even some therapists, priests, and gurus (happily, not the good ones) try to fill up people's empty spaces as if there were something wrong. What few people seem to teach us, or even to know, is

that the hole is real, natural, and everyone has the same hole where we think the self is supposed to be. The hole is there, like an empty cup into which love and joy, life itself, can spill from the universe. There's no room for anything new and beautiful if you have no space for it. And if you fill it up with junk, there's no room for life and the music of infinity to pour in.

— • —

We stuff our minds with trivia just to fill the emptiness we feel.

Ram Dass
Journey of Awakening

— • —

That hole is the truth: there's simply no real 'I' anyway. There's a 'we' in this universe.

Meditation is understanding to good purpose. A hysterical pre-occupation with my*self* is not the same thing as an awareness of the nature and ways of the *self* so it doesn't harm one's own person or anyone else's, physically or psychologically, through words or attitudes. Mental missiles are as dangerous as any other arsenal.

Self-knowledge is merely acquisitive, and ends with the smug, satisfied statement, "I am a person who..." or "That's just me." Thought, for such a person, has invented a self out of bits and patches of memory, stitched together into a construct which reports back to the How'm-I-Doing Bird perched on one shoulder about how well and how far it has got.

Self-awareness, on the other hand, is constant; there is no accumulation, but moves truly with life in each living moment.

— • —

There is no self…the cause of all troubles, cares, and vanities is a mirage, a shadow, dream.

Buddha
The Teachings

— • —

We dislike being with life as it is because that can include suffering, and that is not acceptable to us. Whether it is a serious illness or a minor criticism or being lonely or disappointed — that is not acceptable to us…We need to practice walking the razor's edge.

Charlotte Joko Beck
Everyday Zen: Love and Work

— • —

— • —

All of the insults to our narcissism can be overcome...not by escaping from them, but by uprooting the conviction in a 'self' that needs protecting.

Mark Epstein, M.D.

Thoughts Without A Thinker

— • —

The past exists only in our memories, the future only in our plans. The present is our only reality...We invent earth...heavens... music...arts...philosophy...civilization and science... We mesmerize our children...into knowing they are reality. We throw anyone who does not accept these analogues into an insane asylum.

Robert M. Pirsig

Zen and the Art of Motorcycle Maintenance

— • —

CHAPTER FOUR
Thought And Insight:
Intellect And Intelligence

Thinking is what six billion brains do. Everybody. Everywhere. All the time. You ask a sherpa trekking guide in Nepal, a housewife in Java, a bricklayer in Boise, a Paris dressmaker, a Congolese congressman what their brains are doing, those brains are all doing the same thing. Thinking if they are awake, dreaming (dreams are only unresolved thoughts, unmet challenges, the accumulated, unfinished business of a lifetime) if they are asleep.

Thoughts are the records the brain keeps of its experiences. The brain is constantly recording, not always accurately, everything it experiences. It has records deep inside of experiences, passed on through thousands of generations, of its primeval watery beginnings, its climb out of the earth's oceans onto dry lands, its needs always to feed, reproduce itself, stay alive. It has records of hot jungles and savannahs, of its own primitive fears and exhilarations in bringing kill back to campfires, of the shock and pain of childbirth and death, of its first adored and terrible gods. It has records of vast wanderings, of founding civilizations, arts, taboos, the marketplace, the rules and regulations of belonging to or ejection from the family, tribe, cult.

The complex gifts, if they are that, of words and images reinforce the hardwired motherboard of the generations and constant, continuous recording adds new files that contain your contemporary cultural voices, the voices of your parents and other authorities in your lives, bosses, priests and ministers and therapists and gurus, political figures, movie and television icons, the loving or hateful words you or anyone else said yesterday. What you see on the internet, at the mall, the latest ball scores, music, cars, clothes, all is constantly being recorded, all jumbled in your brain with all the species information collected for millions of years about what is good to eat, what is poison, how to climb trees for fruit, or go into a dark cave for safety, all the cultural and personal information, attitudes, prejudices, taboos collected by your group and by you personally.

Some kinds of thought-records, as we have said, are, of course, absolutely necessary or we couldn't go on living our lives. Some thought-records, equally obviously, only get in the way of seeing what's actually going on around you. These are what poets have called the veil, the curtain, seeing through the glass darkly, what the religious psychologists or metaphysics philosophers simply call the *self*. Or the ego. Or the 'I.'

Intelligence is the brain's second capacity besides thought, and it is intelligence that will tell you what thoughts you need, what thoughts just get in the way. Intelligence. Or insight. Or understanding. Whatever word you like to call the attention you give something when thought is silent, out of the way.

Part of the trouble with thinking is, as we've said, that it gets in the way of intelligence. Another trouble is that thinking itself produces repetitive bad habits, and reinforces old neuronal circuitry in the brain. An example of this is in our relationships — we tend to replicate the same kinds of relationships over and over again. Another example is in our self-talk; we tend to criticize ourselves in the same words over and over again.

- Thought gives a sense of security, a sense of permanence to the *self*, and we so want something permanently secure in our lives.

- The brain is afraid to remain empty. When no new challenge presents itself, it has a bad habit of repeating its thoughts over and over, to keep itself busy. Thinking is itself an escape, and thinking thinks up other escapes in our fear that emptiness is the same thing as loneliness.

- And then the very thoughts and words we continually produce create the walls between each other and the universe that insure the very isolation we say we don't want.

— • —

Coming between us we could see the screen that is formed by those smooth words, those echoes of the everyday we give voice to; the verbal liquid with which we feel obliged, without knowing why, to fill the silence.

Dreams Of My Russian Summers
Andrei Makine

— • —

Haven't you noticed that organizing thoughts and words for something present and lovely transfixes it like pinning a butterfly? Have you also noticed that it is only in the gap, the space between thoughts and words when the mind is silent, that time stops and you're in eternity?

Do you sing to yourself? Notice sometimes that your choice of songs may reflect what you are thinking about. It is informative to pay attention to what we hum, the tunes of our culture that reflect what is stuffed into our brains. There is a song from the play *South Pacific* by Oscar Hammerstein that goes, *"You have to be taught to hate and fear, you have to be taught from year to year, it has to be drummed in your dear little ear, you have to be carefully taught."*

Interesting song.

We are also taught, by our books, magazines, the television we watch (no point in blaming the media, we buy into what we want) that science in our century has or will have all the answers.

We hoped once, and many continue to be taught, that science will solve the problem of psychological suffering.

— • —

...if science has scrutinized human consciousness only recently and leaves other disciplines, if any, to study human thought — then science, which is, God knows, correct, nevertheless cannot address what interests us most: What are we doing here?

For The Time Being
Annie Dillard

— • —

Along with language, what to think about, what disciplines and subjects to respect, what to eat, and how to dress in your particular climate and civilization, what work is appropriate for your class, caste, sex, and position in life, you are also taught both by words and behavior to think the way the generations of your family and friends think. That includes:

- What you are supposed to want.

- What you are supposed to do with your life.

- Who you are supposed to know — and not know.

- What is and isn't important (money, or success, or god, or popularity).

- What you are supposed to remember above all: that you and your family and your country and the times you live in are the most important and meaningful of all and *God is on your side, our side* (It can't *not* occur to the mind with a sense of humor that a Greek or Chinese or Hindu person of a thoughtful nature did not come to the same conclusion 2,000 years ago).

- What group you are supposed to belong to, what tribe, nation, church, political view, or forever feel beyond the pale (we are all terrorstruck at the thought of being outsiders, although being an outsider, not living on a mountaintop, just not buying into general opinion, is the only way to psychological freedom).

You can list the rest of your psychological menu by listening to your mental reactions to any news broadcast.

Your personality is, then, formed out of these groups of thoughts, each one an identity with its own reality: parent to your child, child to your parent, worker to your supervisor, director to your employees, sister, brother, lover, husband, wife, friend, group member. Each has a social, sexual, cultural, intellectual, economic identity. It is easy to get lost in a particular identity in any given situation. Meditation, attention, intelligence lets you pull back, give that piece of you some space, and see that it is only a fragment, and not the whole truth of you at all.

Besides what you are overtly or covertly taught, there are the thought patterns that are formed by the way society treats you. Society may say every one is equal. Ask any inner city person who lives in constant terror over gangs, driveby shootings, drug dealers on corners, crime and violence in apartment building halls and involving their children at school, how fair society feels. Ask any young person from an upwardly mobile suburban family whose words and warnings never match their own behavior, when people say one thing and do another. Do you behave to your children the way your parents behaved toward you? Many parents love their children, and many parents just say they love their children and are really too busy with their own affairs, their own ambitions and needs, their own worries, fears, problems, their own pleasures, to pay attention to their kids. This is true also of the relationships between wives and husbands. We all know whether we feel cared for or not. The problem also is, you can only give what you've got yourself: if you can't feel affection, you can hardly pass it on, and thousands of generations of people making war, killing, terrorizing, tell us there have been thousands of generations without affection for each other or their children.

— • —

We are all looking for sanity and good will in our relationships.
The difficulty is, you have to have a scrap of sanity and good will
to know when you see them in someone else. Krishnamurti al-
ways said, Unless the mind is sacred, you can't see what is sacred.

Ray Fisher
Unpublished Works

— • —

Clearly, you can learn, accumulate knowledge, be a clever law-yer or business person, leader of a gang or a country, you can acquire all the skills and intellectual knowledge in the world — but this will not give you intelligence or skills in living your life happily.

This doesn't mean *not* to be an excellent doctor, mechanic, teacher, scientist, carpenter, businesswoman, or builder. It's important to acquire technical skills, education, knowledge to do what you do well. What we are talking about is not getting lost in these skills as identities. You can be a good anything without being self- important about it. You can be helpful to people, this is a natural thing to do, without making a big deal out of it or electing yourself to sainthood or competing to beat everyone else.

When you find yourself getting stuck in any one of your identities, any one of your various selves (you can rate this by anxious feelings over whether you've made an impression on your boss or your friends, whether you'll get the promotion, the lover, the deal, make the team, the group, the club) you can stop it like a bad dream by paying attention to it in meditation.

Of self-examination, Krishnamurti says:

— • —

The function of the mind is to probe and comprehend.

J. Krishnamurti
In The Light Of Silence,
All Problems Are Resolved

— • —

We often indulge in that waste of time, analyzing and criticizing others because so few are interested in probing into themselves. In self-examination and stillness lies the quality of intelligence that solves problems.

Much violence does not occur when we question what before went unquestioned — not only technical information, but questioning ourselves is an enormous thing. What some of us used to do, what we once thought we had a right to do, smoking, drugging, taking lives, taking slaves — is no longer possible for us because we now inquire into what before it was unthinkable to inquire into.

— • —

...all the Southern land was awakening as from some wild dream to poverty and social revolution...the social uplifting of four million slaves to an assured and self-sustaining place in the body politic and economic world would have been a Herculean task; but when to the inherent difficulties of so delicate and nice a social operation were added the spite and hate of conflict, the hell of war; when suspicion and cruelty were rife, and gaunt Hunger wept beside Bereavement, — in such a case, the work of any instrument of social regeneration was in large part foredoomed to failure. The very name of the Freedman's Bureau stood for a thing

*in the South which for two centuries and better men had refused
even to argue, — that life amid free Negroes was simply unthinkable, the maddest of all experiments.*

William E.B. DuBois
The Souls of Black Folk

— • —

We questioned and continue to question science. It turned
out the earth was not flat. This information made sailing
easier for sailors. In the recent century, we have questioned politics and jurisprudence. This questioning has made access to due
process of law easier for many.

Can we question the structures of our selves? This might make
living easier for everyone.

Just to get this verbally and intellectually is an excellent first
step. But that alone won't change anything. Intellect *gets it*.
Insight, meditation, intelligence, *ends it*, the trouble we cause ourselves.

Stop here for a while. Try an experiment. Listen to your brain
for a day. Carry a small pad and pencil, and make a note every time you hear yourself, your selves, talking to you, criticizing,
directing, having opinions, even just chattering to fill silences and
avoid emptiness. Listen and identify all the different identities in
your head. See if you can even take a shower by yourself without
crowds of friends, your parents and grandparents, dead and alive,
your own various selves — all those different voices, prejudices,
opinions keeping you company, all those slides of your past,
memories frozen in time by thought, keeping you company or
driving you crazy, however you like to look at it. And notice how

all this, like yesterday's newspapers, keeps you from being alive in the warm present, feeling the hot water on your body. What we miss, running our interior movies all the time! What we miss is our lives.

And we waste so much energy.

A sixteen-year-old boy once came to talk to me. He kept getting stoned. When he was high, he invaded houses in his neighborhood, and stole something. Sometimes it was a few dollars, sometimes a piece of jewelry, once even a stuffed dog. At the supermarket he lifted a candy bar, at the music store a CD, not much, and not the point. It was clear from the way he talked about his father, that his father was successful, wanted his boy to be successful, and used both excuses as reasons for his own busyness and how hard he was on his son. The boy felt his father's ambitions: he never felt his father's approval or love. Analysis made it obvious: the boy was stealing things to replace the love he did not get from his father. The stealing went on.

Insight made it clear nothing could replace his father's love. The stealing stopped.

Insight, not analysis, is the factor of change. Intelligence, not intellect, will change your daily life. Insight, intelligence, are just other words for attention and meditation. These can act on all the thoughts, all the fears, all the mental habits you've inherited, all the prejudices, all the false values, and you can see the truth.

You can keep what you want to keep about yourself, and throw away the rest. No need to throw the baby out with the bath water. Just because I once had a jolting insight into how madly my father wanted me to be a writer has never prevented me from emptying my head onto every blank piece of paper I've ever found.

There's nothing, for instance, wrong with hard work, whether you've been brought up to do it or not. But you do not have to step on others to get where you're going. Or ignore loved ones because you are afraid of failure. Or get drunk, overeat, develop a rash because your levels of anxiety are insane, trying to live up to some implanted image.

Spend your time with people you like. We all do. But it isn't necessary to hate, fear, or segregate everybody else.

Our lives are filled with paradoxes and discrepancies: people think one way; talk another way, do and behave a third way entirely. It is easy to see this in others. Watch for this in yourself.

Analysis can tell you why you do things. Intelligence will tell you to stop it if you are hurting yourself or others, or if what you are doing will simply get you nowhere. Most people only see and hear through the lens of what they are, what they already think or have been told by all those authorities we have been taught to rely on as if we were perpetual psychological children. This is not adult, appropriate response, only drummed-in reaction.

Awareness, the maturation of intelligence in the human brain, sees beyond personal realities to the general or impersonal truth.

— • —

Mindful presence helps us let go of preconceptions, hang out in the unknown, respond quickly to unexpected circumstances, regain balance quickly when it is lost, and see new possibilities in situations that otherwise seem intimidating or hopeless.

Ordinary Magic: Everyday
Life As Spiritual Path
John Wellwood

— • —

Meditative awareness is a vantage point from which you can focus on any event from various levels of reality. [There] are habitual reactions...in which nobody really listens; there is merely a mechanical run-off between people. If you are rooted quietly in your awareness, there is space...you see the reaction you would usually make. But you also see the situation in a variety of other ways.

Richard Alpert (Ram Dass)
A Journey of Awakening:
A Meditator's Handbook

— • —

Meditation is not just about creating states of well-being: it is about destroying the belief in an inherently existent self....Insight arises when the thinker's existence is no longer necessary.

Mark Epstein, M.D.
Thoughts Without A Thinker

— • —

Meditation is the ability to stand alone. Not to be isolated: we are a gregarious species. But not to be influenced by the world. It is also excellent practice for death, this disintegration of the self, this not hanging on to what, after all, is only memory. It is like trying to hang on to smoke.

CHAPTER FIVE
Mayhem Or Meditation?
The Structure Of Self

To get away with murder, you have to be found legally insane. According to Barron's *Law Dictionary*, criminal insanity is "that degree or quantity of mental disorder which relieves one of the criminal responsibility for his actions…the person is unable to distinguish right from wrong."

What this means, in our society, is that you have to be psychotic not to know right from wrong, that you are a sociopath if you cannot distinguish good from bad.

Really.

I am troubled by this problem daily. If sufficiently provoked by traffic, an intransigent child, a wayward lover, surliness in boss, friend, aging parent, or the ATM machine, a murderous rage can wreck my blood pressure, fear of consequences can scare me, or I can get depressed for hours, a day, weeks at a time. And how does feeling bad make me behave? Usually badly. I may not murder personally — but I might be angry enough to elect an official who will do it for me, or at least not prevent it. Fundamentally, the mental character of the murderer is not different from our own, even if the neurological or impulse control states are more acutely pathological. In the end, we are all either responsible, or we are all criminally insane. Either all life is sacred, or none is. That some people don't count, so we have permission to behave dreadfully some of the time, is unthinkable. Understanding this, what now?

Who is going to tell me how to handle these everyday matters in my life, show me the right way to live, the right way to go, to be happy in my life, the right actions and attitudes to take so that at the very least, there is less conflict and misery to endure? Who am I to ask, especially since, in the deepest sense, few people have discovered how to live life in the past 10,000 years of what we call civilization?

We have been trained from our long, dependent childhoods to rely on someone else to lead the way, to tell us what to do, and to take the blame when things go wrong. But it seems, this reliance on someone else's view presents some problems.

1. Most people aren't looking for the truth about life, they are looking for someone to interpret life for them and to tell them what to do.

2. Unless you have some understanding of the truth about something yourself, how will you know if another has it also?

3. It isn't really possible to live someone else's wisdom.

What we need when we look into the ways of ourselves and our lives is to stop searching for insight from psychologists and gurus who may have no more insight than the rest of us. What we need is an interest in paying attention, to be awake to the cause and effect of our own thoughts and feelings, our own behavior and its consequences. Most of us will watch a television program every night of the week: with the same attention, we can watch our selves.

The Structure of the Self

The self, you'll discover again, is really a group of selves, all with their own voices, all arguing, in conflict, at war with each other. You have only to listen to your brain for five or ten minutes to discover this. Very quickly, it becomes clear that if we act the way our brains act, according to that inner warring self, we will go on forever producing outer wars.

The path from the inner war of the voices to the outer war, from anger to fighting, is easily traced. We begin by being angry at ourselves for failure. We have failed to be as successful, as beautiful, as rich, sexy, athletic, witty, socially acceptable as we think we should be. Our parents, alive or dead, have fought with us and each other because they too were more full of disappointment in their expectations of themselves, each other, and us, than full of affection. We fight with our children, with our friends for the same reasons. We are all angry because we expect things from ourselves and others we are just not getting. The chronic, edgy feeling people live with daily represents their anger.

All that anger has to go somewhere. We don't usually decide to kill our own families and friends. Triggered by the first instance of external aggravation, such as a personal incident, something seen on television, we are set off, and we take it out in anger at neighbors, at people in the next town, at people of different backgrounds, colors, and countries. War: it begins from inside the skin, inside the home, and spills out.

What if people could actually see and understand this? That war begins in the very structure of the self and its arguing needs and conflicts?

Might each person then handle conflict differently? Wouldn't there be different action?

Action must not, then, come from self. That much seems clear. It must come, therefore, from keeping a close watch on that self and its thoughts and feelings. We must understand that our conditioning, all that we're unthinkingly taught, that we unthinkingly pass on to our children, all the desires, memory of fear, pleasure, pain, the need for approval and belonging, acceptance and so-called love, our opinions, all that experience that creates the hardened core of ourselves and our self-centered activity — we must see that all of this makes up thought. And it is thought that creates the warring selves.

The Bad News

The bad news is, the self isn't going to change. It isn't going to go away. No matter how many books you read, gurus you seek out, no one can take away your self. The more misguided counselors try to muscularize it, strengthen it until it flattens you, but you'll stay away from those who talk about self-empowerment instead of right and mature behavior. What you want is to weaken its grip, even though it is impossible to take a hatchet to it. We've all put our selves to sleep for a few hours with alcohol, drugs, sex, the dark wombs of casinos and malls and movie houses, but always for most of us the self returns.

We know of some who either dissolved or were born without selves: Jesus, Buddha, Lao Tsu, Moses, Mohammed, Brahma, Krishnamurti, and a great many unsung women who were not allowed out for public speaking. The rest of us are still stuck with our egos.

So. What now?

The Good News

You don't have to obey them. You don't have to behave according to those egos, those selves.

You don't even have to waste time trying to change yourself.

You can just change your behavior. Freedom from stupidity begins with changing behavior.

What's interesting here is that as your behavior changes, the pathways in your brain are rewired by neurochemical changes, and you become a different person. But the trick is to act your way into right thinking, since every time our species begins with thought alone, we seem to end up inventing a new technology with dubious consequences.

Anger is a good place to make a beginning with this new, watchful meditation. To watch the self begin to argue with itself or someone else and get angry is an extraordinary thing. There may be some anger at the writer for calling us all irresponsible fools instead of martyred angels, for instance.

Stop reading for a few minutes. Think of something or someone that can make you angry now. In my own case, I am instantly angry when differing opinions threaten my world paradigm; prejudice and ignorance, and the lack of a global view feel more dangerous to me than a loaded pistol, and instead of calling forth in me compassion and sympathy, my banked fires burst into flames. There is nothing like the enraged rush of adrenaline to remind me that thought is a physical, material process.

Scientists can study individual brain cells with a probe: they can monitor the electrical activity of the brain as a whole with an EEG. We know the electrical impulses that involve millions of neurons kicking in and out during the process of thought are carried through the wetness of the brain by chemical carriers called neurotransmitters. The transmitters cross the gaps between neurons, the synapses, to their targeted receptors on other neurons. These transmitter molecules have been isolated in the brains of animals. We have evidence that serotonin and norepinephrine are transmitters involved in depression. Our understanding that the morphine receptor actually exists has allowed us to mediate pain.

In his book *Molecules of the Mind*, Jon Franklin fears that if we do not all learn how our brains work, scientists will plunge unbridled into serving corporate interests, and use molecular psychology in disturbing ways to offer pills that will pacify workers into slavery, create fearless armies of killer automatons, with an artificially activated intellectual elite to run the works.

In some ways this has already happened: patients on maintenance thorazine, the chronic use of diet pills with amphetamines, the once-prevalent use of valium on women particularly who presented with anxiety symptoms — all this represents molecular science at work. Before blaming the scientists and corporate interests, however, we must ask ourselves who is it that wants peaceful women, obedient children, hardworking workers, and a magic fix for every anxiety?

— • —

The chemicals of curiosity flow in the brains of scientists, and...as an observer of this new science...I can't offer any suggestions to prevent this. We couldn't stop this science even if we wanted to, and given its power for good, I for one wouldn't want to try. [But] the science of man is far, far too important to be left to the scientists.

Molecules of the Mind
Jon Franklin

— • —

The point of understanding molecular psychology in your own mind, is the perception that human thought, emotion, and behavior are chemical, quantifiable processes.

We'll assume you have got yourself angry with something by now. Pay attention to your body, to what is happening to your adrenal system and its store of dopamine, norepinephrine, and epinephrine. The adrenal glands are intimately connected to your emotional states, and secrete accordingly, creating fight or flight responses. With rising levels of these chemicals, you can feel your face flushing, your heart pounding, your head throbbing with the rush, maybe your fists or your mouth or your stomach clenches. It is the chemical epinephrine that mobilizes the body into its intense need to run away or punch something. If your anger creates pathologically excessive secretions, and hypertension, excessive sweating, tachycardia, headache, anorexia, personality changes result — a host of cardiovascular conditions may occur.

Can you continue to sit and just watch these physical symptoms happen to you and do nothing? Anger sends chemicals rushing through your system like a triple vodka or a lidocaine injection at the dentist's office, and like any roller coaster ride, it isn't over till it's over. Like any other chemical reaction, anger will pass even if you do nothing. I find this interesting. I always thought I had to do something to bring a roll of anger to an end. Turns out, all I had to do was wait it out.

You can experiment with this yourself. See if the next time you get angry, you can let it pass. Time it on your watch. With some people, anger is a fast burn, rises and passes quickly. With other people, anger is a slower rush and takes longer to pass. You may find your anger is a personal reaction to any provocation, and has less to do with the type of provocation than your own chemical processes.

The more you understand about your own molecular psychology, the more freedom you have to act as you prefer rather than according to the winds of the world. Experiment, not with analysis — most of us by now have read enough books, experimented with enough support groups, therapies, watched enough talk shows to know that just being a human being in this increasingly hostile world is enough to make anyone permanently annoyed — but with this fascinating kind of observation. So, not only see if the next time you get angry, you can let it pass, but see if your action is different, more appropriate, more effective. After all, we've all discovered that lashing out at people we love produces more guilt and embarrassment than satisfaction. And as we've already examined, pent-up personal anger only leads to collective war. So do see if the next time anger rises, you can just let it happen, feel it, let it go by without doing anything about it.

This does not suggest passivity: it suggests more effective, more appropriate behavior is the reward of meditation. Thrashing about with flailing arms and the tongue flapping in the wind leaves one looking silly or dangerous, and people more under control either laughing at you or approaching with handcuffs and a straightjacket.

There are those who feel:

1. Changing human nature isn't possible: that we are genetically programmed to behave in certain ways; that we are a genetically aggressive, xenophobic, male dominant species, and that is that.

2. If God wanted us different, he'd have made us different.

3. I'm one of the top dogs and prefer to leave well enough alone.

Human beings are an adaptive species. Adaptation is our greatest survival equipment. But in humans, adaptation may arise either genetically or nongenetically through cultural evolution. Our species evolves both through genetic programming — and cultural learning. As Stephen Jay Gould makes it clear in his book on human intelligence measurement, *The Mismeasure of Man*, we are the result of biological potentiality, not just biological determinism. Our gross biology as large animals keeps us grounded rather than on the fly like insects; we are born helpless (many organisms are not), we do not photosynthesize, we age and die — all of this according to a broad range of genes and genetic behaviors that interact with the environment.

— • —

Wide behavioral ranges should arise as consequences of the evolution and structural organization of our brain. Consider, first of all, the probable adaptive reasons for evolving such a large brain. Human uniqueness lies in the flexibility of what our brain can do. What is intelligence, if not the ability to face problems in an unprogrammed (or, as we often say, creative) manner? If intelligence sets us apart among organisms, then I think it probable that natural selection acted to maximize the flexibility of our behavior. What would be more adaptive for a learning and thinking animal: genes selected for aggression, spite and xenophobia; or selection for learning rules that can generate aggression in appropriate circumstances and peacefulness in others?

The Mismeasure of Man
Stephen Jay Gould

— • —

Many people who study the human condition agree that thought is a less-than-accurate measure of the truth of anything. Quantum physicists, scientists, metaphysical thinkers, philosophers have all stated clearly that not only does thinking **not** make something so, *but actually changes what is seen.* We have all begun to learn that the observer affects the observed; is, in fact, the observed. I see what I am programmed to see and thereby change what is seen. The 'I' who is doing the looking, the imagining, brings along its own maps, processes, baggage, its own binoculars, its own lenses, through which it sees what it is looking at. Of course, this distorts the picture. In physics, it can be demonstrated that the watched is changed by the watcher. Read any article on light as particle or wave. In psychology, anyone can prove the same thing. This is why there are generally so many different stories told about the same event. We have problems processing actuality even when we know better, because recorded memory as thought gets in the way of empathy for the facts. A good example is that while I know thought has invented the 'me' it still feels as if there is a 'me' and I keep interpreting the world according to the 'me' instead of what actually is.

— • —

Worlds are created by brains...At a simple level, bees, migratory birds, dogs...contain internal maps of their surroundings. Humans, who think abstractly, create more complicated...maps going beyond their own surroundings, to include the world, celestial objects, real and hypothetical beings, and the past and future as well as the present...Making world models is a familiar human activity."

Reality and Empathy: Physics, Mind,
and Science in the 21st Century
Alex Comfort, M.D., D.Sc.

— • —

In our culture, we call this activity religion or science of a sort. These are often our ways of making up the world as we go along, whether thinking makes something so or not. Then we pass all this along to the next generations (instead of teaching them the art of observation for themselves), as if — if we can get them to believe our theoretical worlds — it validates us and what we say.

The trouble is, that just because a million people believe something, it doesn't make it right or true. Remember when the ancients thought the world was flat? That women had no souls? That children were owned by their parents? That the sun went around the earth? That only birds and pterodactyls could fly?

But as Richard Burdon Haldane says, "Nature [include human nature here] may not only be odder than we think, but odder than we can think."

Our perceiving system is the human brain. And this organ, we now know, has its problems.

The point is that the observer is involved in everything observed. And the observer, the 'I', the self, is limited by its own memories and information, its own fears, rages, desires, needs, recorded impressions.

Now: can observation take place without the observer? Can my eyes watch the birds feeding at the small feeder just outside my window among the sunlit, newly-bloomed daffodils without further comment? Can I watch my daughter's face without registering my pride in her, my memory of quarrels, past expectations, future plans? Can I see anything, anyone at all with new eyes, fresh vision, without opinion, as if for the first time? Just see, nothing more. Personally, I am forever saying to myself, "It is not necessary to have an opinion here. So don't have one. Let something, anything, just be."

Biologically, as we've seen, the human brain has another capacity besides thought: it has this capacity for simple observation, insight, awareness, intelligence, whatever you like to call it, as part of its adaptability to various environments and conditions. The brain may not be able to annihilate the self, but it certainly doesn't have to act according to the self's directives. Just because the self wants something, doesn't mean it has to have it. Just because you want something doesn't mean you have to give it to yourself. Just because you feel something, doesn't mean new congressional law has to be passed or stars stay their course. Interesting freedom, isn't it, not to have to make high mass out of yourself? To be free of the bondage of yourself and all your voices is a blissfully peaceful way to live.

Remembering those questions at the beginning of this section, that people always ask about the point and the purpose of life in general, their own lives in particular, what the Dalai Lama, the exiled spiritual leader of Tibet, says, is that it is to be happy.

By happiness, it isn't meant that we get lost in one passing, superficial pleasure after another whether that's an ambition to be rich or Mother Teresa, drunk on power or being in love. Happiness is the state of taking care, being awake, aware, watchful of life internally and externally all the time.

- So we don't turn temporary pain into long-term suffering for ourselves or anyone else.

- So we understand that thought has its proper place and we do not let it spill over from the technological arena into the psychological arena.

- So that we see the world and its people with new eyes every moment, not through the filter of the past.

- So we can see that suffering depends on how we react inwardly to outside events, not on the outside events themselves (these can cause pain, of course, but we don't have to keep suffering over pain, the past).

- So we can see it's our own brains with their fears, angers, cruelties, memories that cause the suffering, not the gods (a volcano is the earth erupting, and it's true that if people's houses are in the lava's way, they will burn, but this is no more personal than you or me belching, and there's no point in confusing nature's activity with the extraordinary glory of the universe many people call God).

Thought or Insight

We all have the intelligence to use one or the other as the situation requires.

1. Thought, the response of memories, with its knowledge, the contents of consciousness and intellect — is the PAST.

2. Insight is always perception in the NOW.

3. Thought is TIME — not time by the watch or the time it takes to commute to work — but psychological time as past and future.

Insight takes place now. You can always have insight, because it is always now.

The Dalai Lama's point is eminently sane. The whole point of life is the joy of living (remembering that happiness and just pleasure are not the same thing). People breathe out what's inside them, and if people are full of meanness and misery, that's what they give off. And as we've said, the world does not need the pollution of any more foul breath.

— • —

Meditation is not a matter of trying to achieve ecstasy, spiritual bliss or tranquillity, nor is it attempting to become a better person. It is simply the creation of a space in which we are able to expose and undo our neurotic games, our self-deceptions, our hidden fears and hopes.

Chogyam Trungpa
The Myth of Freedom

— • —

The truth shall make you free.

John VIII, 32
The Bible

— • —

Our chief concern is the transformation, the radical change, of the human mind. The human mind includes the brain, the heart, the organism as a whole, the mind that has created this world around us, the world of corruption, violence, brutality, vanity, and all the structures that bring about war...This change cannot possibly be brought about without knowing oneself, self-knowledge.

J. Krishnamurti
Total Freedom

— • —

Section Two

MEDITATION

CHAPTER ONE
What Is Meditation?

Meditation is to see something with new eyes, not through the I of a thousand yesterdays. The I of us is those thousands of yesterdays: new eyes are needed to see that we must not be living monuments to the past with its divisive myths. Meditation is the watching myself, the listening to those ancient directives. In the watching, divisions between me and the world cease, there is the glorious rush of connection, like falling in love, being out of yourself when the sky, the ocean, the sunlight over a mountain, the game, the lovemaking, the moment is perfect. It's that state when there's no separation between you and another, you and the sky or the wave, the field or the light.

We've all had these moments. These are the moments when there is no feeling of separation and loneliness, and you feel at one with the entire universe. Meditation is what happens when thought, with its self, and its problems, stops, and there is only attention.

It is meditation to see that it is simply not true that we are alone, that our particular congregation of molecules is alone in the universe. It is meditation to see life as it is; that we don't exist in a vacuum, that each of us affects everything around us by contagion if nothing else. Good is also catching, as well the plague. So it would seem that this absolute truth we all seem to be seeking is simply good harmony with life. Life with all its complexities is the truth, and when one has solved the problems posed by life, one has found the truth out about living. One's own life, that is.

It is meditation to see that life is relationship. Even just standing around we are not in a vacuum alone, we are in relationship to the air we breathe, the ground we stand on. And it's the perfect way to see oneself, in relationship. Our relationships are the perfect mirror, the best process of self-revelation, the clearest way to see ourselves. In the action and interaction of relationship between

us and the people and things in our lives, to property, to social position, to marriage, to money, to society, to church, country, family, possessions — in all the attachments we form and extend like a spider spins its web — in all this, we can see our own neediness, even greed, with all its self-defending fear.

Understand this process, and you understand the structure of psychological thought. The problem is, as long as one depends psychologically on people and things, neediness and fear grow; one grows desperate to hang on to what — or who! — you have, to fear its loss.

Obviously, natural needs are not greed. We need to breathe, food to eat, the general company of our species. It's only when things and people assume undue psychological importance that there is trouble. We all love certain people better than others, certain foods, a particular house. But to see that we all live in terror of losing what we have, including our lives, and that living in fear of loss makes one chronically nervous if not desperately unhappy, is a truth perhaps more useful than trying to justify material greed, power hunger, and ambition of position as righteous.

This is meditation. To see it like it is. And to see that in you is all humanity. If superficially specialized, we are all profoundly alike in that our long-term suffering is not so much a question of external conditions, but lies in the very nature and structure of ourselves.

It's often painfully embarrassing, always a shock and a surprise, every time I discover I am the author of my own discomfort. But the discovery of the cause — me! — so often eliminates the discomfort, it's worth the embarrassment. And I've found seeing myself in action and thought on a daily basis gives me a good laugh.

Stop here, if you like, for a breather, and try this out for yourself so you don't take my word for it. Close your eyes and sit quietly for two to five minutes, give full attention to something that hurt your pride or your feelings, made you feel insecure, angry, jealous, greedy. Don't try to fix the feeling, ignore, drive, or sweet-talk it away. Go into it by finding out what directive inside your head made you think you needed something enough to be upset when you didn't get it, anything from a good opinion to a new shirt. Constant alertness like this either dissolves discomfort pretty quickly or allows you the insight that it is simply part of your nervous response and will pass as your life flows on.

What is it that suddenly requires some of us to stop in our tracks, announce to the heavens or the bathroom mirror that we aren't living right, that something is wrong inside, and it is suddenly necessary to reevaluate, to find something more important to give life meaning than the right car or clothes or position?

It isn't usually a walk on the beach among the dune roses. Usually, it is an intense crisis of suffering. Or the emptiness of a lonely life even among one's family and friends. Suffering makes one intense, sensitive, aware. It is in the intensity of pain that you are able to face yourself as you are. When your life hits raw nerves, you can listen better. The weak, when they are in pain, want consolation which, like any addiction, only grows stronger by what it feeds on. The strong want the truth, the right way to end pain without hurting themselves or the people around them.

The human brain so far has based its systems for living on security. The trouble with security, as anyone can see, is there isn't any. You can always lose it all, and our lives are demonized by this fear.

The I of me is millenniums old, and if this I born of thought hasn't seen through the veil by now, it is time to use the brain's other instrument besides thought: attention, insight, awareness, the still small voice, that receptor to intelligence of the universe we all possess that replaces the blindness of self-absorbed fear with at least momentary vision of what truly is going on to make the human brain suffer so much psychological pain and anxiety.

There doesn't seem to be any point in saying, "Well, I'll give up my self." That's like creating ideals. I am at liberty to create whatever idea I want. But if I look, I am still what I am. Afraid. Anxious. Driven by this or that need. Lonely. Dependent. Frustrated.

So, seeing this, I stop trying to do anything at all about my brain. I see how my brain works: it is one way, I want it to be another and I try to push it around. I am angry; I want to be calm, and so forth. When I see nothing changes, then what? The mind stops trying. It is quiet. My mind stops fighting itself. When the brain stops fighting itself, even for a minute, something new happens in that gap between conflicting thoughts.

Just leaving a space for the universe, insight, god, whatever you like to call it, to come into your mind, will bring new action. And new action rewires the brain, changes its neurotransmitter paths.

This state is not transferable from one of us to another. You can't buy it from an analyst or a guru. It has to happen to you — you have to sit quietly for and by yourself — for you to see what happens and how your life can change in the light of silence.

All we know is the past, our conditioning, cultural, personal, so forth. To see something new, it has to shut up, all that inner chatter telling us what to do and not, when and whom to like and not, what god is and not.

When the past noise is quiet, then maybe we can find out what love is, to live without fear, to see that the only security is to learn to live without it.

For the brain to give up its roots in the past is frightening to think about. But we won't know psychological freedom until we try it. It's like leaving home as young adults to make new homes of our own, to write our own scripts for living. Only when we're on our own is it possible to deal with what comes up when we're on our own: fear can't be provided for ahead of time. We won't know until we've tried it what it is like to live without the dependencies that cause our sufferings.

Living in prison, we talk about freedom.

Living as an American or Russian, as a member of this or that sect, party, social class, we talk about brotherhood. From behind barriers, social, economic, national, religious, we speak of humanity toward all when these very divisions are the cause of war outwardly as our own inner conflicts cause disease inwardly. To live in harmony, the barriers must come down. And we must stop driving around in our own personal tanks, shooting out our own personal opinions, gazing malevolently out from our own private turrets.

Don't you feel, most of the time, or at least some of it, that there is the feeling of calling out to another, to the world, from inside the well-defended box of the self we all live in? Don't you wonder why, after all the thousands of years of holding one another during sex and parenting and friendship, we are still without intimacy, so the ground goes on shifting and opening up black holes under our feet?

The bliss of meditation is connection, the end of separation, of black holes, of the terror of total isolation. With the art of meditation, you can stop the loneliness and its terrors. Drugs are artificial, temporary, eventually dangerous. Meditation is natural to us all. We've just never been shown the way. The way can be as simple as sitting down, back straight so you can breathe properly, and keeping the mouth closed. Watching the breath coming in and going out, watching thoughts and letting them go by instead of getting lost in them, arguing with them, pushing at them. This exercise works better than any artificial means, works most of the time, and leaves no addiction or destruction in its wake. If sitting still is difficult for some, nature walks work. A nature walk does not have to mean summiting Everest or trekking wilderness and coming home with a bear attached to your leg. Somewhere, anywhere in nature will do, with your back straight, your attention inward, quiet.

Everyone has been in this silence at one time or another. It can make some of us panic and rush right back into the old, familiar rooms of our mental selves. But by trying these practices, it is possible to tolerate silence for longer and longer periods, even to tolerate the presence of whatever demons come up, and stay out there for more time each time.

Meditation is found in silence, which doesn't mean turning off children, the city, the music next door. It doesn't even mean just not talking to other people or yourself. It is the gap between thoughts, total attention when the self is absent.

Krishnamurti says it best, to my mind.

— • —

Meditation is the movement of love. It isn't the love of the one or of the many. It is like water that anyone can drink out of any jar...it is as though the mind enters into itself...

The soil in which the meditative mind can begin is the soil of everyday life, the strife, the pain and the fleeting joy. It must begin there, and bring order, and from there move endlessly....You must take a plunge into the water, not knowing how to swim. And the beauty of meditation is that you never know where you are, where you are going, what the end is.

J. Krishnamurti
Meditations

— • —

It turns out meditation is not separate from daily life. It is not just going off to a mountaintop or to a specialized retreat; any tree is Buddha's tree, any lonely place, Jesus' wilderness. It is not just sitting in a corner and saying some magic words, mantras, or prayers, and coming out to behave in the same possessive and aggressive ways. It is paying attention to everything you do in daily life, everything you say, how you behave, what you are thinking. It is taking time for walking or sitting in silence so your life can be reflected in the pool of that silence. In silence, the universal intelligence can be heard, sharing truth with you, giving you insight into how to handle your feelings and problems. Only in this silence, when there is no interference from all the voices of the selves, can you hear without the static of all your brain's tape-recorded announcements. In silence, oneness with everything is possible, and an end to fear, anxiety, loneliness. It is like holding hands with love. That the moment doesn't last doesn't lessen its blessing. It's somewhere you can always return.

The ability for meditation and silence is not just the property of priests and ministers, yogis and rabbis, shamans, saints, and other holy women and men. We all have this ability in our brains. You've been there often enough to know this absence of self already, in moments of crisis when someone else needs you, when a burst of energy is required, when you've suddenly had the feeling of coming back to yourself after the crisis or the movie or the game is over. If you've come back, it means you've been away for a while.

Meditation is arranging for time out, off duty, free.

CHAPTER TWO
The Many Ways To Meditate

Coming Down

Meditation, attention, is a built-in capability in all of us. Once you're there, it's easy. What is difficult, really difficult, is getting to that state of mind. It is truly hard, in our speeded-up, competitive, constantly busy, be-a-player-stay-alert-and-on-top-of-it-or-stop-for-a-moment-get-left-behind-out-of-the-game society, to stop. We are so trained, so conditioned to emergency states, to the sound of continual red-alert alarms, that to come down off the adrenaline rush is hard on the nerves. It can feel like the screaming of tires when you suddenly brake to a stop at a stop sign. Whether the inner screaming is over the children, work, illness, a low golf score or a high performance review, the neurons in contemporary brains fire at furious speeds and in constant panic. As Ted Koppel would say, 'Genuch.' Enough.

Easier said than done. Most of us need some techniques to begin to meditate. There are helpful ways to begin to meditate. Because first you need to quiet the brain and body so you can meditate and give some attention to your own state of being instead of the demands of the world. We are programmed always to be doing something: to do nothing will produce a few seconds of distress before it brings you ease. When you get into quiet sitting, you will feel connected to your own rhythms, the rhythm of life, connection to the rhythms of the whole universe. When you are into the quiet sitting, you will come to a relaxed place to sort out thoughts about your self, emotions and feelings, healing the hurts and aches of the day, of the past. You will understand what amends need to be made to others, what daily or whole life adjustments need to be made for yourself. You will feel renewal of energy, rested and alert. This will happen whether you sit for five minutes or five hours — if you remember that meditation is not relaxation but an alert attention to all that passes inside and outside of you. You do not work to empty your mind: you watch your brain's thoughts, feelings, inner workings. You watch what you do all day long: it takes sitting still in silence to process, to sort out, to clean your mental house.

Meditation is as natural as breathing. For most of us, in our noisy culture, to get the nervous system quiet so meditation is possible is the difficulty. No matter how well we understand that a thought is just a brief, tiny electrical event or a 'bit of undigested potato,' it feels like an imperative to clean the kitchen or save the world now.

— • —

Of course, if I want to make the world a better place to live in, I have to do it from the inside out, not the outside in.

Ray Fisher
Unpublished Works

— • —

Getting In

For those who find instant sitting in a state of choiceless, nonjudgmental attention impossible, there are countless meditative practices from chanting to mantras, from breath-counting to yoga, dance, martial arts forms to lead you in to your inner world where you can embrace instead of beating yourself up. The choice of ways to quiet the body to quiet the mind are various and many.

For some people, simply reading and following what is suggested in this book or other meditation books such as those listed at the end are enough to get started. For others who are more active or prefer company, want variety or further teaching or dialogue, there are retreats, spiritual or religious, organized group dialogues, centers, abbeys, foundations, schools, institutes, also listed at the back of this book.

No other places are necessary but your own place. No other teachers are necessary but your own deeply interested attention. You can simply be aware of what you like to do in your own life and begin there. If you are good at simply sitting down and doing absolutely nothing but watching your thoughts unfold as if on a television screen without trying to control or judge them, you are already meditating and don't need to read another word of this or any other book. Most of us need help getting there. If you like to read, begin your journey into stillness with reading, Krishnamurti or the Bible, Buddhist teachings, the Hindu *Gita*, the prose of W.E.B. Du Bois, Chief Seattle, a Walt Whitman poem, the Tao. If your nervous system is the result of an active gene pool or you are personally too frayed to sit down right off, begin with a walk, yoga or other stretch postures, a bike ride, gardening, a swim, or learn one of the attentive martial arts, kung fu, taikwando, tai chi, sufi dancing. Turning on with your own mind and body is a high better than turning on with alcohol or gambling or love affairs, or off with drugs or television. The author has done most of them, and can vouch for this scrap of sooth.

This is a partial list of techniques and rituals, to be described more fully in the following pages, that can lead into meditation:

1. Sitting meditation.

2. Walking or moving meditation: hatha yoga; tai chi; one of the martial arts; Japanese or English rituals of serving yourself tea or coffee ceremoniously and slowly; flower arranging; a sport practice in slow motion, as in repetitive golf or tennis swings; slow, attentive housecleaning, carwashing, gardening.

3. Breathing practice, either prana yoga or zen practice, for example.

4. Relaxation techniques.

5. Singing, chanting, mantras (a mantra is any sound that resonates in your brain when hummed aloud: this can be anything from devotional, Jesu, Allah, Amen, OmManiPadmeHum, to personally meaningful, a loved name, the computer search engine Yahoo!). Stop reading for a moment and try one: the experience of vowels hummed aloud massages the brain. Just try saying hummmm aloud, holding the sound in your mouth and up in your nose and down in your lungs, even lower in your belly, and you've got the soothing point of mantra.

Prayers and mantras, rosaries and davening, puja, Buddhist, Hindu, Native American offerings and chants, Catholic masses and Jewish or Protestant services, incense, candles, pipe ceremonies, prayer wheels, ancestor and nature worship — anything, everything can help to quiet the brain's noise. But the whole point is not the ritual or technique itself (relying on the technique itself is a useless form of trickery that will leave you hopelessly untransformed a year, five or twenty years down the road), the whole point is eventually to integrate the mindfulness of sitting and moving meditations into general attentiveness in your daily life, to yourself and how you are living out your days. This is so you can change your anxiety into calmness, tolerate the outrageousness of life without its hurting you, so you can wear the world as a looser garment instead of a hair shirt, so you can acquire duck oil, and the pains of daily life can roll off your back instead of jabbing you in the throat, groin, and solar plexus. **After** all, the word roots of attention and tenderness are conjoined: if you begin with tender attention to yourself, you will extend it to everyone and everything else.

Meditation Is Not A Toy

Meditation has side effects.

- Extra energy: physical; emotional; sexual.

- Or a laidback feeling at first, just the initial relaxation of your nerves and muscles.

- Resistance: this may take the form of boredom, and boredom is just a form of resistance, in the beginning, a 'why-am-I-doing-this' voice running frantically around your brain making you feel silly as well as bored, or nagging you with to-do lists, production schedules, food-marketing, all the usual. Pay no attention, resistant voices will fade as the strength, ease, and balance of your own life force takes effect.

- Anxiety, nervousness, difficulty just physically sitting still in the beginning. This often happens, not only to athletes and the physically active, but to those who chronically resist making themselves comfortable. Give yourself the comfort when you sit of appropriate temperature, straight back, easeful posture, a cushion, a bugless, telephoneless, childless atmosphere, and watch without obeying the calls to action — stay with your sitting the way you would walk through an aching muscle — your system will eventually quiet down.

- Ecstasy, extraordinarily blissful highs.

- Memories and hallucinations, aural or visual (you may at first be visited by your past, joyful, sad, or old memories in the form of demons that haunt lovingly or terrify). A different set of chemicals sets off electrical currents in a meditative brain that may create new, recent, or old images, sensations, smells, sounds (memories and images as well as inner voices are why many people find it difficult to keep themselves company, so sit somewhere you feel safe in the beginning, in your own closet or your favorite movie theater).

- Speed — you may feel your brain speeding up, your heart pounding, your nerves jumping.

- CLARITY, INSIGHT, CONNECTION, COMMUNION, INNER BEAUTY, LAUGHTER, PEACE, HARMONY, COMPASSION — these are the most lasting and vivid side effects.

Sitting Meditation

Right now, you can begin meditation, if you would like to try the experiment.

First, walk around your life until you find a quiet place: your bedroom; the front steps or the back stairs; the bathroom. Try the city park under a shade tree, the woods near your house, a corner of your garage, a car, a beach. An alley will do, or an empty classroom, or office cubicle — anywhere you can be alone (meditation is not a time when you want to feel assaulted by outside stimulation any more than attacked by inner selves), and quiet for five, ten minutes, half an hour, to lower your eyelids, go inward, inside yourself. A patch of sky, a bit of green, a ray of sunlight, something not human-made is good to be near. A lit candle is fine. The moon or sun is better. The light, the bit of sky, or something green and alive are an extra benediction. They are not absolutely necessary. Even external quiet and solitude aren't totally necessary. I've seen people in meditative states on airplane flights and subway trains as well as under floating clouds on mountaintops.

What is necessary is to sit somewhere, and to sit quietly.

Sit on the floor, in a chair, on the stairs, under a tree. Sit with your back straight, not rigid, shoulders down away from the ears. You can sit cross-legged or in lotus position, or if you are on a higher seat, have your feet flat on the floor. Do not lean against a wall. You cannot carry a wall with you through life to lean on. Sit as if your butt and your back were a comfortable and supportive chair. Once you learn to sit well, you'll return to sit in your body like a familiar and welcoming chair. Relax. Relax, not collapse, as yoga instructor Marlene de Santo informs me every Thursday evening.

Stillness is important. Physical comfort contributes to the ability to sit still. Make all the small adjustments necessary until your body is as comfortable as your quiet place. Fidgeting distracts from attention. Keep the whole body, even the eyes, still. If you are facing a lovely scene, a garden, or the sea, take a long look around first, thank the world for its beauty, and close your eyes. Or you can lower your eyelids slightly, if closure affects your balance or sense of safety, and focus your eyes on a spot six feet in front of you. Now be still. It is in this stillness lies the sound of truth, what some people call 'the still small voice,' and others call conscious contact with god or the presence of the universe — and the greatest high you have ever known. It is in this stillness that personal troubles, needs, cravings, mental wanderings, mental nonsense as well as deep pain and sorrow arise and push each other aside for your attention with rapid speed. Psychological hurts from childhood arise, fears and attachments arise. But also the flowering of intelligence, the watchful attention that sees through these, and in the moment of insight, ends them. For the moment, insight ends them. For most of us, the problems and character defects soon return. But there is always more stillness for personal troubles and the troubles of the world to fade away.

Breathe, and keep the attention to the breath. When your brain wanders off, bring your awareness back to the breath. Watch your thoughts as they follow each other through your brain, but don't let any of them run away with you like wild horses or beat you up in the back alleys of memory. Don't reject or censure, approve or congratulate your thoughts. Let them enter, let them go. After your sitting is over, you can sort them out and see what interests and occupies your brain. (There is nothing like a quiet sitting to get to know what is really going on in your life. Your main concerns will pop to the surface like corks in water.) For this small, silent space of time, just watch the parade and come back to your breath.

In one form of Buddhist sitting meditation, the breath is breathed in to the count of five, and let out slowly to the count of ten. In another, ten in-and-out breaths are counted and the count starts again. If you lose your place, it means your attention has wandered. Start again. In yoga meditation practice, eyes are closed, or attention is on a spot six feet in front of you, perhaps on a lighted candle, on a loved object, on simply a stone. To lose sight of the object results in a loss of concentration. The whole point of any practice is actually not meditation itself, but to quiet the mind so thoughts slow down and finally stop and the silent gaps between thoughts lengthen. Again, the trick is not to avoid thoughts or make an effort to control thoughts. The trick is to watch your thoughts instead of thinking them, to see what you think about so you know what concerns you, not to analyze those thoughts during your sitting. Just let the thoughts happen — if you don't bother them, after a while they won't bother you.

The trick here is, there is no romantic, mysterious, exotic trick. There is nothing to do but nothing. Have no expectations. Do nothing. JUST SIT. Sit for only four or five minutes to begin with. See what happens. Eventually, sit for longer periods of time, twenty minutes, even forty minutes. As usual with sitting, there are no rules, just sit, attend, and see what happens to you so you can see what happens to you

— • —

The state of mind that exists when you sit in the right posture is, itself, enlightenment....There is no need to talk about the right state of mind. You already have it

Shunryu Suzuki
Zen Mind, Beginner's Mind:
Informal Talks on Zen Meditation and Practice

— • —

— • —

Once you have decided how long to meditate and where, you don't have to decide anything else.

> Lorin Roche, Ph.D.
> Meditation Made Easy

— • —

The ultimate aim is to bring mind and spirit together with the body in perfect unison.

> Ron Van Clief
> The Manual of the Martial Arts:
> Introduction to the Combined
> Techniques of Karate, Kung-Fu,
> TaeKwonDo, Aiki Jitsu for Everyone

— • —

Trains of thoughts and feelings that might pass through your mind, remembering that some thoughts will be deep, some passing, some light, some frightening, some funny, can drive through your brain with such varying speeds and intensity, tone and mood and texture, it can feel like bedlam — especially if you have agreed not to control but only to watch. Be affectionate with them. All these thoughts, feelings, images are yours, are you. They might go much like these at first:

- What am I doing sitting here when there is so much to do?

- The breeze feels good, the floor is hard, my nose itches.

- Got to finish accounts, pick up the children, stop for milk.

- We haven't had sex for a month; am I getting fat?; how often do other people have sex?

- Was I really a bad child? I was a bad child, no I wasn't, so how could they do that to me?

- I'm bored, so why was it I'm sitting here?

- Wear odometer for run, wear what to the boss's cookout?

- Do my children have ADHD or just my own lack of discipline?

- Does everybody in the office hate me, or do I just hate myself?

- It's peaceful, lovely, sitting here in my inside world away from out there.

- What will happen to my brain if I go on drinking this much? What will happen to my social life if I don't?

- Am I doing this right? Am I breathing right?

- The world is in a mess, I'm in a mess.

- I'm tired of being angry, I'm tired of being uncomfortable in my skin.

- Where are you God when I need you?

- Isn't the light suddenly marvelous....

Many people have reported altered states of consciousness, paranormal visions, half-forgotten memories, terrifying childhood nightmares and experiences reexperienced, demons long forgotten ringing in their ears, at first. People have also reported dull lists of tasks, possessions, errands. Many are confronted with sexual thoughts and feelings, rageful thoughts and feelings, all unwanted confrontations of images they stay busy to avoid. Many people on the other hand report beatific visions, scenes of enchantment, the presence of immortality, a profound communion.

The artist, my friend Claire Dunphy, who thinks of herself as just a moving scrap of earth, ends her breathing meditation in such a communion.

— • —

To be as a river
To be as a tree
Always a channel
Of love from heaven to earth
Earth to heaven

Claire Dunphy
Chants

— • —

Whatever comes up for you, all of it is just you. Nothing attacks you from outside. There is nothing, in just sitting, to fear.

— • —

I will recognize whatever appears as my projection and know it to be a vision...I will not fear the peaceful and wrathful ones, my own projections.

Chogyam Trungpa
The Tibetan Book of the Dead

— • —

In your sitting meditation, fantasies, fears, memories, thoughts will continue to flow through your brain. Whether you have done yoga postures, readings, focusing, breathing to quiet the body, you have now stopped, you are quiet. You are not hanging on to any thoughts or ideas, you are letting them go by, watching them like clouds floating by. This is meditating. You're doing it. If you grab at any of the fantasies or memories, or you analyze or problem-solve, you are doing the harder work of the sorting process we call thinking again. Let go again, and again you're doing that simpler thing, meditating. Over and over your mind may get caught on your thoughts, some sound, plans. Just keep letting go, flowing on, and bring your attention back to your quiet sitting, your breathing.

This is the beginning of meditation, of the silent mind.

It's the best way in the world to know yourself — to see what is on your mind. Not get involved with it, just see it. What is going on with you will become clear. And this self-awareness is the key to freedom from the suffering the self causes. Attention, it turns out, not control, is the way to change your self, and therefore your life.

As you get more practiced, you will discover that you can bring any problem, any question about yourself and your life, into your meditation, not to think about, solve, or analyze, but to drop into your silence like a quarter in a slot — and listen for, not think about, the answer. You can find out what interests you to do with your life, what to know about anger or fear, how to handle situations, by asking the universe, in silence, a question, and in your altered state of consciousness, in silence, to learn the art of listening for what comes to you.

People have been listening in this way for thousands of years before you. Their writings are quoted throughout this book to keep you company on your own inner journey, and are further listed at the end.

Walking and Other Moving Meditations

1. Mindfulness, attention to slowing down a special everyday activity, making and pouring tea, gardening or mowing the grass, feeding a pet, arranging a few flowers, showering in the morning, going to bed at night — doing all or any of these slowly, ceremoniously, attentive to each detail is a good meditative practice.

2. Relaxation techniques, physical ones. Few people can just go limp. Tense and clench every muscle group in the body, suddenly let go. You can do this lying down, standing, sitting in a meeting.

3. Stretches: yoga stretches have been done effectively for thousands of years by women, children, and the Marines.

4. Walking: communing not only with nature, but silently with people, the traffic, the noise, whatever passes you by. Neither embrace nor shut anything out. Just walk.

5. Chanting, singing, dancing, prayer.

6. Devotions, visualizations, mantras.

7. Mindfulness in everyday life to everything you do.

Mindfulness is just doing the things you do with complete attention, to your life and the people in it, the activities, the food you eat, the air you breathe, the work you do, your favorite chair, the music you hear, the birds you see, the children. All that is part of your life actually happens to you instead of just rushes by in the blur of getting it all done, getting through the day, getting the list behind you.

If your own life doesn't happen to you, what will?

So much of what we do every day, we do mechanically. We use the computer and travel cyberspace without blinking an eye at the extraordinariness of technology. We have all had the experience of driving somewhere, walking, flying, riding the commuter train, and arriving without knowing how the time passed. It all goes by without our being conscious of it. We don't want to arrive on our deathbeds, look back at our lives, and say, "What was that?"

Eat mindfully. Walk mindfully. Lie down, get up, speak, do your work mindfully, with full attention to what you're doing. It will make everything in life more meaningful. So much in our lives seems to be either boring or stressful, but sometimes I wonder if that isn't because I am boring and stressed-out rather than life itself. Just stopping to contemplate that the air I'm breathing is an actual gas rather than just a nothing I'm taking in to my body, and that its molecules are in blood that is running furiously around inside me, puts the adventure of life back into my sense of things. Another contemplation I do is remembering that death is only a word we have invented, that everything in the universe came from and breaks back down into stardust, that our atoms will exist until time's end. Puts me back in touch with eternity and the flow of things, instead of leaving me stuck, lost in temporary frustration and blur. Some people use the Serenity Prayer, or the prayer of St. Francis for contemplation, or get on their knees, or salaam.

The physical and mental paths mentioned are all wonderful preparations for the inner silence of meditation so that insight instead of rush and panic can flow. You will discover there isn't a need to think all the time, have opinions all the time, and since there isn't a need, you can try not having any once in a while. It's very difficult not to like this, dislike that, want this, not want that. It's very difficult to center yourself at first. It gets easier.

- Paddle a kayak.

- Run a mile.

- Dance to any music for ten or twenty minutes.

- Play the piano, a guitar, a flute, a harmonica, listen to someone else do it.

- Chant, hum, or sing, say a mantra or prayer. For an excellent variety of these, read Ram Dass' *Journey of Awakening: A Meditator's Guidebook*. Read the Bible, St. John of the Cross and other saints, Thomas Merton, the Bhagavad Gita, the Upanishads, the Koran, Buddha's teachings (Dhammapada), Lao-Tsu's *The Way of Life* (Tao), the I Ching, African and Native American teachings, Rumi's Sufi poems.

I like to remember always, though, what St. Therese of Lisieux said: "I felt it better to speak to God than about him." And I would add that a silent openness to the universe is as much prayer as a dialogue with god.

- Read about meditation. Especially read the great minds and religious philosophers and teachers like the contemporary Krishnamurti. His *Total Freedom*, and *The Book of Life* are full of daily meditations. Try collections like *Ordinary Magic: Everyday Life as Spiritual Path* edited by John Welwood for a good representation of contemporary writings on meditation. William James' *The Varieties of Religious Experience* is a classic.

- Do ten minutes of martial arts or yoga exercises or positions or forms. If you don't know any of these, there's no mystery about them. There are plenty of instruction books. Try Richard Hittleman's *Yoga: 28 Day Exercise Plan*, with over 500 step-by-step photographs; Ron Van Clief's *The Manual of the Martial Arts: An Introduction to the Combined Techniques of Karate, Kung-Fu, Tae Kwon Do, and Aiki Jitsu for Everyone*, also with photographs of forms and techniques.

- Do zazen, or sitting exercises. Read *Zen Mind, Beginner's Mind, Informal Talks on Zen Meditation and Practice* by Shunryu Suzuki.

What I'm suggesting here in the above points, is that not only is there no great mystery to meditation and meditative exercises, but you can learn them for yourself, in your own time. There is no need to run out and sign up with some guru. Yoga and martial arts classes are good for those who want or need the discipline, who prefer group exercise. But with all the books and videos out there, and even morning television instruction, you can do all this on your own.

- Write or read poems, particularly by poets like the great African American poet Langston Hughes who understand human pain, the kind that torments most of us.

— • —

Because my mouth
Is wide with laughter
And my throat
Is deep with song,
You do not think
I suffer after
I have held my pain
So long?

Langston Hughes
The Dream Keeper

— • —

The poet Edna St. Vincent Millay wrote:

— • —

Thus in the winter stands the lonely tree,
Nor knows what birds have vanished one by one,…
I only know that summer sang in me
A little while, that in me sings no more.

Sonnet

— • —

Meditation is possible even in your sleep, when the subconscious sorts out and pays attention to our deepest conscious concerns. On waking, examine your dreams, remembering that it is your associations, not someone else's theory, that will disclose your dreams' content.

— • —

A dream is the answer to a question we haven't yet learned how to ask.

Fox Mulder, alias Chris Carter
The X-Files

— • —

The ability to pay attention, to be in a fairly constant meditative, aware state of mind, is the greatest tool in determining whether what you learned in school, from your family and culture, what you hear now, at work, in the media, from family, friends, in political, religious, sexual, relationship discussions — in short, what you witness — is true or false. After all, we are all subjected to what Robert Persig calls in his book *Zen and the Art of Motorcycle Maintenance* "mass hypnosis — in a very orthodox form known as education."

So when you are eating, walking, working, reading, thinking, moving, or relaxing, simply be aware that eating, walking, working, thinking, moving, or relaxing is happening to you.

— • —

Just let things happen as they do. Let all images and thoughts and sensations arise and pass away without being bothered, without reacting, without judging, without clinging, without identifying with them…That's what we are — a sequence of happenings, of processes, and by being very mindful of the sequence, of the flow, we get free of the concept of self.

Joseph Goldstein
The Experience of Insight

— • —

The great discovery that you will make in meditation is that events are simply the result of cause and effect, even if we can't always figure out the exact causes or can't see far enough through the fog ahead to know all the effects of what is happening right now. What a tornado is *not*, however, or a broken leg or an ended love affair or a child's illness, is an act of a personally vengeful god who's got it in for us. The point is not to confuse acts of physical nature, even when these cause pain and disruption, with the intelligence and order of the universe. Just as scientific investigation traces the causes of volcanoes, tornadoes, floods, meditation will give you insight into the causes of your troubles — in your choices, your selves, your conditioning, your attachments, your ghosts and voices. The uncomfortable news is that it is usually we ourselves that cause the trouble, either from inattention or misguided motives. The good news is, it is certainly easier to fix yourself than some unknown, uncontrollable power, human or otherwise.

We have all discovered a lot of life is good, stimulating, often beautiful and rewarding. A lot of life also ranges from dull and irritating, to pure hell, outer conflict, inner torture, and total chaos. With some patience, tolerance during initial discomfort, experimentation in practice techniques to get yourself into a silent stillness, you may discover that meditation works better than mayhem in solving your own and therefore the world's problems.

CHAPTER THREE
When To Meditate,
Where, With Whom

J ust as there is no mystery about the ways into meditation —
although extraordinary mystery happens sometimes once
you're sitting — there are no mystical rules about when to go inside yourself. Meditation, that watching the back and forth flow
of outer and inner worlds, can happen anytime. Just as it's easier
to get a breath of fresh air when you sit near an open window, it's
easier to meditate when you are sitting somewhere quiet with
enough time to be quiet in. All you can do when you are flying
around is notice you are flying around. And stop.

Some people prefer to take time out before the day begins, to
prepare for the day's rush: a few stretches; a reading from a daily

meditation book (myself, I just leave one in the bathroom); a quiet silence. Some people find the evening better, after a busy day, to prepare for the evening (I have a friend who says it gives her a whole new start on the second part of her day). Some people prefer the day's end; a few exercises before bed, quiet time, and sleep. There are people who take a little quiet time several times during the day for a quick inventory of mood, feelings, thoughts, an invitation to the heavens for a blessing. Great preparations are not mandatory or necessary. Just stop what you are doing, stretch, breathe, sit down, hush, and OPEN YOUR MIND TO WHATEVER COMES INTO IT.

The where to meditate is equally unmysterious. You don't actually have to go anywhere to meditate except inside yourself. But sometimes it's nice to leave the noise and dailiness, even the quiet corner where you usually sit to ponder over your life, and go into retreat where others are doing the same thing. Among other reasons, human beings are a sociable, curious species, and we all seem to like knowing how other people do whatever they do and if they are doing it the same way we are doing whatever we are doing.

There are meditation centers, retreats, monasteries, convents, yoga groups, zen temples, Christian, Jewish, Muslim, all kinds of meditation centers, martial arts and tai chi schools, meditation schools, seminaries, institutes, and foundations without end to choose from all over the country, all over the world. You can go to India. You can sit in your back yard. Some facilities are listed at the back of this book, and you can find nearby centers in your telephone book. Ask your local rabbi, minister, priest, yoga, or martial arts teachers for suggestions.

Even in retreat, there are no secrets, no magic rituals, no special places, no experts. It's just people, sitting, going inside themselves, giving themselves space to understand the workings of their own self which is the same as other selfs, reading their own book of life, so very much like everyone else's book of life.

The whole point of meditative silence, of giving the mind the room to go over the details of your life is that you are able to learn for yourself whatever you want to know about the contents of your consciousness. You are able to learn for yourself that while there is something divine, something holy, it most certainly is not the collection of anxieties and aches thought has put together as the 'me.' You can't live on someone else's truth second-hand: you have to discover it for yourself. In Alcoholics Anonymous it is said you can't get sober on someone else's sobriety — you have to stop drinking yourself. This is true revolution: to learn life for yourself. Rebellion is just a negative blueprint, a reaction to someone else's truths, not freedom.

Anyway, you must have discovered by now that no matter how right someone else is, until you've discovered it for yourself, it continues to sound like only hollow opinion.

Obviously, the business of truth is not a matter of doctrines and rituals, or even always the vast business of god and the cosmos. Truth has to do with everything in everyday life. With a revolutionary attitude of finding out for yourself, you can even discover whether you're really hungry at dinner, really love sports or cooking, cars or babies, or the rest of the things your friends say they like, or whether you've simply been told dinner is what people do at six o'clock, it's abnormal not to watch football, love the kitchen, or pant over new cars and babies. What other habits and attitudes are part of your psychological inheritance, your educational system?

We have been told what to think instead of being taught to think for ourselves, so many of us go through the motions of our lives thoughtlessly. Prejudice, greed, ambition, escape from our own pain through drugs, gossip, stories, sports, war, the devouring of our children's, lovers', other people's lives, dependence on approval, all of this we have absorbed from our culture and continue to pass on to the next generation — without a thought. We've learned it, and we pass it right along at home and at school, mixed right in with tooth-brushing, bed-making, history both national and familial, Aunt Martha's apple pie recipe and Uncle George's knack with hammer and nails. What are we thinking of? Or not.

Part of the problem even in talking about meditation is that we have been given so many preconceptions about it. We have as many preconceptions about it as we have about religion, or god. Thousands of years of accumulated opinion (another word for scripture) have separated us from very source of our lives. There is no gap between us and the universe or god or religion or meditating. It is as natural to the human heart and psyche to think about and doubt and struggle with these matters as it is to breathe. Matters of the human spirit are not a question of being 'good' or 'nice' (I've known some perfectly rude spiritual people, and some perfectly charming gangsters) or even of giving money or your time to those for whom life has been less kind — this is a natural activity, no great virtue. Their writings tell us that even the holiest of monks and nuns, gurus and high priests struggle and doubt and question in meditation just like the rest of us.

Following another is only imitation in the hope that someone else will do the work of saving you. Meditation, silence in the presence of the universal connection, is available to anyone. It is simply a question of self-examination and behaving ourselves so that our lives have meaning and beauty and purpose instead of that dreadful, dragging undertow people sometimes call despair. And it is about being a light to oneself.

— • —

A light to oneself! This light cannot be given by another, nor can you light it at the candle of another...The very investigation to find out what it means to be a light to oneself is part of meditation....To go into the question of meditation, you must be wholly, inwardly free from all authority, from all comparison, including the authority of the speaker.

J. Krishnamurti
This Light In Oneself:
True Meditation
Edited by Ray McCoy

— • —

What is meant is a warning: most books, teachings, lectures, groups, sects are more interested in proving they are right and the only path, that the leaders are something special, than with showing everyone how simply to sit, go inward, and listen and find out for themselves what comes to them.

— • —

Don't be a Kool-Aid drinker.

Ray Fisher
Unpublished work about
The Jonestown Mass Suicide

— • —

Truth is a pathless land.

Why do you want to be students of books instead of students of life? Find out what is true and what is false in your environment with all its oppressions and its cruelties, and then you will find out what is true.

J. Krishnamurti
The Book of Life: Daily Meditations With Krishnamurti
Edited by R. E. Mark Lee

— • —

The whole point is that we must see with our own eyes and not accept any laid-down tradition as if it had some magical power in it. There is nothing magical which can transform us just like that...There is a great attraction to the short cut.

Chogyam Trungpa
Meditation in Action

— • —

Beware of false prophets.

Matthew 7:15
The Bible, New Testament

— • —

Those truths being pondered, and with the understanding that outer forms and disciplines, rituals, techniques, and exercises are not the point, it can be wonderful fun and very healthful to take physical yoga classes, stretching, breathing, relaxation, sitting, in a retreat like Kripalu or Esalen or a good local yoga center with a good teacher. Yoga is and has been for four thousand years the ancestor on which calisthenics for sports, aerobics, gym exercises, military boot camp drill, and contemporary video workouts are all based. It can also be an emotionally and spiritually deepening experience—as well as an initiation for the psychologically shy — to do sitting meditation in a group in a Buddhist zendo, a Christian retreat, a Jewish yeshiva, a Muslim temple, a Hindu ashram, a Native American vision quest. It is a restorative mental vacation to go on retreat with a church or camp group, to join a chanting or singing or prayer group, spend contemplation time at a monastic retreat or spiritual center of any sect or denomination of any religion. You need not be a purist. You don't have to subscribe to beliefs or enlist in religions or sects to sit in a cathedral or enjoy the quiet of sacred places.

On the other hand, you can do all of this, of course, without leaving the house to go to a class. Relaxation techniques, yoga exercises, tai chi, all are available now on video for housebound moms, working women and men in home offices, the socially fastidious. Go it alone, or invite a friend or two and start your own group to reinforce your disciplines or just keep you company. Remind yourself and each other that proper breathing to oxygenate the brain and relax the muscles of the body is important: rushing breathlessly through relaxation rather defeats the purpose. You might take into account for your nervous system that attention might also be paid to cleaning up what you take into yourself along with good food and fresh air: what you watch on television, listen to on the car radio, read, what you do with your time, what you talk about. Negative gossip, trivia, both spoken and listened to, are equally as toxic to the brain as a dose of a bad drug. Again, it's not so much a question of behaving in ways that are good of you but good for you. As that ancient holy man said, "If you want to be holy, be careful what you put into your holes."

You can try this exercise and see how hard it can be to change even one habit. Notice what you have attached your senses to. See the difficulty of giving up one violent television program, a sports event, Hollywood or neighborhood gossip, your favorite ice cream or junk food, criticizing anyone for just one day, buying something you don't actually need.

One pitfall I've discovered is trying to imitate someone else's act. My favorite is Mother Teresa — lots of good works and a bestseller. I've learned that someone's life cannot be borrowed from someone else any more than a wart. Anything you have been doing thoughtlessly and decide to stop doing, from giving up eating dead animals to saying no to the next drink or act of discourtesy, is difficult. But it is infinitely easier to do so from your own conviction than it is from someone else's.

In discovering that some of your old habits are just holding you back from the life you want to live, you may also discover that some of your companions change, that even your relationships with family and old friends, while not lost, are different. It is not so much that you will reject them for not keeping up, but that they will push you away for having insight they haven't had yet, for having health and peace they may envy.

— • —

Your kinsmen are often farther from you than strangers.

Ali

Maxims of Ali

— • —

But while these losses will hurt, consider that your power of example, especially for your children, may plant more mustard seeds than you know. Your children will, after all, emulate what you do later if not sooner, rather than do what you say. Seek comfort from those traveling on the path beside you as you climb up your new mountain toward new horizons.

Deepening your meditation and getting on with a more generous, kinder life, to yourself as well as everyone else, is the best antidote to the depression and confusion, the feeling of being stressed and overwhelmed in the face of the outer world and those inner voices. Naturally, just sitting around silently breathing isn't the cure. It is what you find out about yourself and life while you are sitting there breathing that's the curative. Among the lessons we all learned when we were young was that the world wasn't the way we thought, solid and forever. Rather than solid, it is fragmented, broken into atoms and molecules, and impermanent, always changing and in flow like a river. We discovered early, that trying to hold our arms around a world we'd made up hoping to keep it all together, was like trying to hold the river in our arms.

Some of us took years to stop trying, to stop our maddened attempts to control not only outer events but our inner environments. Most of our addictions, after all, are only attempts to control our inner worlds, revving them up against downers, turning the temperature down when we threaten to boil over. Letting go of controlling — not of your behavior — just the world, the future, other people, and all the other weather you are powerless over, is what allows the space, breath, insight, and time to behave properly anyway. We keep acting as if we're not going to die. We are. There's some freedom in that thought if we approach it right.

It is we who make up our own universe. Whatever happens, good or bad, it is we who make up our own reactions to the events. A friend of mine said, we even make up our own parents: they were what they were, and all the children in the family turned out according to their own, if differing, interpretations of them. Meditation discovers all this.

Clearly, then, meditation does not mean sitting around drifting any more than relaxation means going limp and collapsing. Whether in sitting silence or in action, it simply means WAKE UP AND PAY ATTENTION!

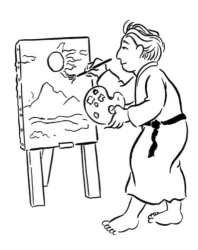

— • —

Calmness of mind does not mean you should stop your activity. Real calmness should be found in activity itself.

There is no particular way in true practice.

Shunryu Suzuki
Zen Mind, Beginner's Mind

— • —

By their fruits ye shall know them.

Matthew 7:15
The Bible, New Testament

— • —

Jesus spoke of compassion. Buddha taught freedom, not of, but from the self. The Indian Saint Kabir and the Western Saint Theresa yearned for the love of and connection to god. Lao Tzu and Confucius and Matthew talked about right living. Intelligence is always the same, at any time, in any culture, any caste, class, gender. It is always discovered to be the same thing. When 'me' is here, life is small, full of fear, often full of attitude and aggressively vicious. When 'me' is not here, and there's only tender attention, the world opens wide.

It's only a question of turning the eyes into windows, not mirrors.

Section Three

MAYHEM OR MEDITATION: YOUR BRAIN CAN SAVE OR KILL YOU

CHAPTER ONE
Fear

I'm sad. I'm afraid I won't be happy any more.

I'm in love again. I'm happy. I'm afraid it won't last.

I'm hurting. I'm afraid the pain won't ever go away.

My whole world has dwindled down into the dark and fractional size of my pain. …I'm afraid it won't be big, bright, and beautiful again.

Finally, I have my house and some money put away. I'm afraid of losing it all.

I'm afraid something will happen to my children.

I'm in my thirties; I'm afraid of what's happening to my sex life.

I'm in my forties; I'm afraid of getting old, getting sick, growing helpless.

I'm in my fifties, and suddenly I'm afraid of dying. My parents died, and I'm next.

My skin is aging. I'm afraid my husband will find a younger woman. I'm afraid my wife will stop loving me if I lose my potency.

I'm afraid I don't really exist, that someone will find out I'm a fraud just hoping to god I can get from one moment to the next.

I'm afraid of the long, deep hell of depression I have felt in my life returning ever again, that I won't be able to run fast enough to outdistance it, far enough to escape it.

All those psychological fears are thoughts. Physical fear, protecting yourself in the face of harm, rushing from a fire or the path of a train, isn't fear; it's biological intelligence. Fear of something that isn't happening yet or isn't really life-threatening is just thought. Is psychological fear ever necessary or useful? Sometimes we call this kind of thought 'worrying.' There's even the notion in some of us that if we do enough worrying, this alone will ward off the evil. Fear is based on memory of past hurt, that it will come again. Attention to what you are actually doing in your life, not worry, prevents painful fears. Meditation will bring you this attention.

No one picks up a book like this about meditation who is feeling perfectly comfortable. Only people like you, and me, walk around their lives muttering questions like: what is this thought-invented self that keeps pushing at me, that is full of irritating habits and anxieties, that sets me up and puts me down, keeps me awake nights and drives me through my days? We can see there is no such entity as a self. We can see that the self is a construct of bits and pieces stitched together from memories by thought, an illusion invented by thought, full of gaps and holes that prove clearly that the self has no continuity. Every time it goes to sleep or gets distracted, it wakes up again and pulls itself together in fear for its life.

What am I to do? Why is it so haunting a loneliness, this notion that I don't exist, that I am a made-up dream put together by thought? When I stop taking emptiness personally, understanding that we are all empty, that we are all empty together, it is easier. I have a moment's peace. Then thought with its fears of isolation and suffering returns.

We are all afraid of one thing or another all the time. The whole job of the self is to protect itself, rightly or wrongly to keep itself alive, just as the whole meaning, the whole job of life is to stay alive. We are all mostly interested in ourselves, in our lives, our affairs, our prestige, our satisfactions. We are interested in getting what we want out of life. What we are afraid of is not getting what we want, or losing what we have and not getting more. So we fear death, not only of the body, but of the very selves, the egos that are giving us all the trouble to begin with. We fear loss of reputation, popularity, approval, the people and things we depend on, our friends, money, jobs, a place in the world as well as a house to live in. We fear darkness, loneliness, inner emptiness. We fear authority, certain people. Our problem is that we are ashamed to admit our interest is 'me first,' and so we never admit and face our fears.

The fact about fear is that as long as there is a 'me' — and for most of us this lasts our lifetimes — fear cannot be conquered, it can only be understood. It cannot be vanquished forever, it can only be seen when it occurs, and an insight into its cause will dissolve it until the next time fear rears up.

Fear is one of the great problems in life. It makes us behave badly, causes prejudice and hate, conflict in families, crime in homes and street, war between nations, and in the microcosm of our bodies, cellular war —mental and physical illness. Fear makes us step on others to get what we want to feel safer, to steal materially and emotionally from others as if more of something out there could protect us. Actually, nothing out there can protect us from fear. But if we know what we are afraid of, and the cause of fear, it is easier to get beyond it whenever it occurs. Often, it seems, it doesn't occur to us that we even need freedom from fear. We keep seeking relief, an unending, all-consuming, and always fruitless quest.

Like anger, fear is chemistry-based. Next time you are psychologically afraid, why not experiment with recording both the physical sensations, the rush, the rising of adrenaline, the feelings in chest and stomach and head, noting the rise and fall of fear physically as well as the thought-content of the fear itself. See if attention exacerbates or diminishes the fear.

Mark Lee, director of Krishnamurti Publications America, just telephoned to remind me that Krishnamurti once said we must treat fear like a precious jewel, as it is the great teacher.

Fear is a troublesome emotion in our society. Men are told it is unmanly even to mention it, and even strong women have a certain contempt for fear. We stuff or convert into anger or isolation the fear and its doppleganger, shame, instead of what is more helpful: to look at our fears with curiosity, affection, attentive understanding, so we can learn by watching our brains as closely as a computer monitor or television screen what those fears tell us about ourselves and our social and inherited conditioning.

Bad Habits

Much of fear is based simply on bad habits of thinking, of incorrect interpretations of past experiences and incorrect suppositions that what happened before will happen again. We may fear a new relationship or a new job, for instance, without even truly understanding what went wrong in the past except that it hurt. Thought itself, based in memory, produces bad habits of thinking.

It is interesting to note that if you are not thinking, you are not afraid. You can try this for yourself: focus on a tree, take interest in a child, or watch a bird intently even for a moment — thought stops, and with it fear.

But the brain seems afraid to remain empty When no new challenge or entertainment presents itself, it has a bad habit of repeating its thoughts over and over and over, to keep itself busy, so busy that nothing new, unknown (we are terrified of letting go of the known, like a child its parent's hand), creative or original can enter. Yet it is in the unknown that the answers to our problems can occur.

This is why constant analysis, constant thought, produces nothing in the way of solution. There is nothing new in thought. It is always old, based on memory. To find the new, we have to shut up. In silent attention to a problem, new insight can occur.

Otherwise, the brain repeats and repeats and has an obsessive quality, chewing over and over its own cud. All to keep out the new, the unknown, to hang on to the old and familiar, even if the old and familiar thoughts are full of pain. They are at least familiar. They are at least busywork to take up the time. Like television noise. Fruitless, but occupying.

— • —

The mind continually objects to living with suffering and so escapes into various activities it calls pleasure. But pleasure ends and there is more pain. Is this happiness?

J. Krishnamurti
Reflections on the Self
Edited by Raymond Martin

— • —

That the past, represented by frozen thought, is no place to find out what is valuable insight into the present, is represented well by the Muslim holy man Idries Shah, well- respected for his wisdom. When people asked him the foundation of his holiness, he invariably answered,

"I know what is in the Koran."

"Well, what is in the Koran?" a fool asked him one day.

"In the Koran," said Idries Shah, "are two pressed flowers and a letter from my friend Abdullah."

So, habits and memory are just functions of thought. If you are not thinking, you are not afraid. We won't confuse intelligence, the intelligence of physical survival, with fear. We all have enough sense of physical preservation to jump out of the way of a Mack truck coming at us on the highway. But psychological fear for the preservation of the self, that habit of sitting around being afraid when you are really perfectly all right, just is not necessary.

What Do You Fear?

To make a beginning, you have to find out what it is you are personally afraid of. To make a beginning, you have to go through, not around, but through the feeling of being ashamed of fear, of being afraid to find out what you are afraid of. It is time for meditation.

Sit Quietly

It's hard to hear anyone or anything else — and impossible to listen to the music of silence — if you're fidgeting around and talking to yourself. Go to your meditation place, make certain it is warm enough, perhaps light a candle or stick of incense to create a pleasant atmosphere, and sit, cross-legged, in lotus position if you can, for perfect balance, back straight, shoulders down. Relax, as my yoga teacher says, but don't collapse.

Do some deep breathing from the belly, air in to the count of five, hold the breath for a count of ten, breathe the air out slowly to a count of ten. This oxygenates the brain, calms the nervous system to make it easier for the body to sit quietly. Close your eyes or focus them on a spot a few feet in front of you.

The next time you breathe out, make the sound of OM or AMEN aloud in the comfortably lowest tone possible, so it resonates in your head. Hold the note for a long as you can breathe it out. This further quiets the system.

Now that you are inside your mind, drop the word fear in there. Find out just sitting there, what you are most fearful of.

Do not think, or make lists.

Just listen to yourself. We tell ourselves, as others have told us, what to think. We have a habit of talking to ourselves all the time. Learn to listen to yourself as you would listen to a little child on your lap trying to tell you something.

What are your fears? The superficial ones may surface first. What are your deepest fears? It is not necessary to admit them to anyone else, but at least admit them to yourself, let them emerge slowly through your mind chatter until you can hear them, taste them, know them so you can know yourself better. They may be similar to those at the start of the chapter. There will be more. Some may date back to your childhood, some may be more adult.

- Something bad will happen to my children, to my wife, husband, lover.

- Loneliness outwardly, inner emptiness; no one will love me.

- Being attacked, out there on a dark night, by someone entering my room.

- Going blind, or deaf; illness, being in a wheelchair.

- Getting old, growing helpless mentally, physically.

- Not having enough money to meet the bills.

- Sex: fear of losing my sex life to define me as desirable.

- Being nobody, past my prime, without position or respect — not mattering.

- Death; being alone in some dark, forgotten corner of the universe.

- Pain: emotional as in depression; physical as in torture, beatings, rape.

- Cancer, heart attack, stroke, AIDS, a family genetic disease.

- Job loss, layoff, demotion.

- Failing relationships with friends, lovers.

- Loss of approval, popularity, reputation.

- Fear of facing yourself as you are, frightened and ashamed like the rest of humanity.

- Closed spaces, high places, silence, fast motion, open spaces, falling.

- Heaven, Hell, God, known guilt, unknown guilt, being found out, being betrayed, being watched by whoever is ticking off your faults.

A fear we all share, a particularly silly mental habit, is the fear of what we don't know. Of course, what we're actually afraid of is losing the familiar, the safety of the known. A good example is our fear of loneliness. We don't spend time alone because we're afraid of it, and so we never find out there's nothing to be afraid of. Death may be the same thing.

My own greatest fear is that life should turn out to be meaningless after all. But if I am willing to sit, in the way we have been discussing, this lifts. Once in a while, the center as 'me' vanishes — there is only a floating attention — and the universe fills me like sunlight in a glass cup with a miraculousness some people feel they must name. And this light, this flowing toward me of the universe is meaning enough. Then I know that there is something beyond all this suffering, and my fear disappears. When fear returns, I sit again.

You have just done a meditation. Take a deep breath and stretch your body. Know that there are no marks in meditation. Half of fear is this habit of comparison. Did I do it right? (According to whom?) Did I do it well enough? (Compared to whom?) If you learned something about yourself, you did fine. Even if all you learned was that it is difficult for you to sit still. As we said, this happens to people in our driven, restless society. So keep trying, until you can sit still just for two or three or four minutes. Even short meditations are better than no meditations at all, and the time periods will increase with interest, like every other interest.

What we all need to remember is that this business of waking up and paying attention to our own mayhem is not only for the enlightened few. Anyone not in a coma can do this. And great teachers are not necessary for meditation the way they are to learn brain surgery or the art of the bowling ball. In meditation, you are your own best teacher, and sometimes the only teacher.

Know what you fear.

Insight into fear— this will change fear itself by changing the neuronal activity of the brain cells that are making you suffer.

— • —

Mere book-learning, however profound and extensive, or doing rare and apparently impossible deeds, does not enable one to obtain true enlightenment. Ask such a scholar or hero, "Do you know yourself?" He will be constrained to admit his ignorance.

The guru is one who at all times abides in the proud depths of the self.

Ramana Maharshi
The Teachings

— • —

For everything there is a season, and time for every matter…a time to be born, and a time to die;…a time to keep silence, and a time to speak….

The Preacher in Ecclesiastes 3:17
Old Testament, The Bible

— • —

CHAPTER TWO
Anger

The behavior of the human race is probably conditioned by anger based on fear more than any other motive. Anger is often called by more socially acceptable names: healthy aggression; a competitive spirit. Even in bringing up our children whom we say we love, anger based on fear for them or fear of being found to be bad parents drives our disciplining their behavior more than the simple teaching of needful lessons.

Angers are not only based on our personal fears. Our brains hold memories of the whole, long history of our species, whether we are aware of those ancient memories or not. As a species, we have been and remain violent predators. It's a fact. Prey have eyes on the side of their heads; predators have evolved with eyes in front that work in concert. We deal with infringement of our territory for the most part not with flight, but with fight. You cut me off in traffic or hurt my family, I get angry. You take something I think is mine, my car or my lover, I get angry. You just get in the way of my opinions on a hot day, I get angry. And anger in a predator can turn nasty. It becomes aggression.

Because anger is a chemical reaction in the brain and glands, it starts a chemical rollercoaster in us that begins with a rush. This all of us can notice. What we don't see is that this chemical roll of anger will subside on its own eventually and come to a stop — without our having to take any action at all.

Now, can I see it, this rising of anger and not act on it? Or at least, can I not act out on it until the chemistry subsides and I can consider clearly what is to be done? It isn't a question of allowing someone to hurt your child or your sweetheart, or take your lawnmower or insult your ancestors. But if what I do too quickly is kick you, you'll kick me back. If I get my friends to help me, you'll get your friends, and we have group, gang, religious, national war on our hands. The trouble is, children and other innocents get killed in the crossfire. Children who survive learn by imitation to behave in the same aggressive ways.

By not allowing yourself to act the instant you get angry, you allow time for clarity of purpose, a change of view. Animals are violent: humans are violent animals (we have a history of thousands of years of war and slavery to prove this), but we are animals with a difference — we have the ability to look at ourselves and change our behavior. It isn't necessary to invent an attitude or preach some ideal of nonviolence — just to see the violence in oneself and let it go, not do anything about it. Clearly, if you see some lunatic beating up or chaining a woman or child, you put a stop to it as you would put out a fire in a burning building. You don't have to think twice about it. But the ordinary daily angers based on personal fears, of being taken from, frustrated, dis-counted, unable to control things, these can be considered and reconsidered before any appropriate action is required.

Your own meditation will show you that anger is often a reaction to being hurt, particularly in our pride, in some image we have of ourselves as smart, attractive, powerful, important. Notice further what we have been conditioned to do about it, if not directly by our parents, by the society and media we have created. We have been taught that as we are hurt, to hurt others — or even hurt ourselves. We have been programmed, if not to use guns and knives, to use our behaviors and mouths to be cruel. We stonewall in silent treatment, sulk, or we rant and rave. If we are too frightened of losing approval or our personalities are too restrained to attack others, we attack ourselves: drink too much, drug; eat too much; blunt our senses with television, gambling, sex.

Books and magazines and reporters talk about righteous anger. Is there really such a thing? People talk of crimes of passion, killing from so-called love, so-called honor, and in Washington D.C. there is invariably talk of killing-for-peace. Has love got anything to do with possession, jealousy, pride, killing? Has any war ever put an end to war? Or is all that stuff just self and its extensions warmed over! An excuse to vent angers built up over generations, over traditions, over national histories and personal living.

The trouble with anger that goes unexamined is that thought turns it into resentment and it burns ourselves and others. Resentful anger, like acid, corrodes the cup that holds it (people actually get stomach pain from anger, because anger literally releases acid into the system). And it does not matter whether you are angry just at one person or everyone. Being rageful may feel better temporarily, engender more energy than being hurt, for a while. Certainly it covers over the shame some people feel when feelings or pride are damaged. If another man takes my wife, or my best friend takes my husband, if my book doesn't get published, or my cake win first prize, if my child fails in school, or I'm overdrawn at the bank, I feel shamed. It feels better to get angry and blame someone, gives me more energy than the depression of shame and hurt. So I have to deal not only with the original hurt, but also the victim's shame. Together, shame and hurt can make anyone furious.

What am I to do about it?

Many people need initially to let off steam, with a long walk, pillow-beating, some time out. The most important tool you have now, is your sitting meditation. When I am dealing with anger, I find that in order to sit quietly, I have to do breathing-stretches first.

Stretch Exercises

STRETCH UP.

1. Stand, feet together, back straight, hands at sides.

2. Begin deep inhalation (abdomen expands), at same time raise arms out at sides and bring overhead, palms together, raise up on heels and s-t-r-e-t-c-h up toward the ceiling, feeling your ribs lift up out of your pelvis — hold for slow ten count.

3. Slowly back to starting point, exhaling.

4. Inhale and roll down, exhaling, lower chin to chest, slowly continue to roll down, feeling your spine's vertebrae bend over one at a time until your face is as near your knees as possible, stretching backs of legs. Hang down, arms and shoulders loose and relaxed, for ten.

5. Spread legs wider than hips; head, shoulders, arms loose. Don't forget to breathe slowly in and out.

6. Close legs, feet together, inhale and roll up slowly.

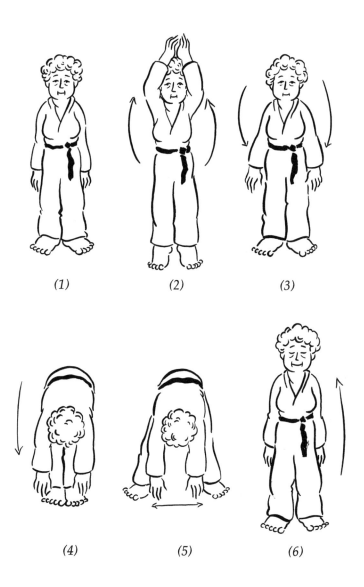

(1)   (2)   (3)

(4)   (5)   (6)

Sit now in your comfortable silence position, do a few more deep breaths slowly, a few OM's or AMEN's, and drop the word anger into your brain. What usually makes you angry? What is making you angry now?

- Hurt pride, loss of approval, love, friendship.

- Loss of job, position, respect, feeling bullied.

- Money problems, theft.

- Physical pain, helplessness, cruelty to yourself, to children or animals, others.

- Being told or made to feel inferior in yourself or because of your background.

- The responsibilities of a successful adulthood, the shame at any failure, being given or having to submit to authority.

- The past; the future as the result of the past.

Now that you know what angers you generally, and what particularly angers you right now, wait for the rush of adrenaline to subside, then decide to do something effective about your rage instead of burning yourself and everyone around you in the conflagration.

— • —

The right means is action which is not the outcome of hate, envy, authority, ambition, fear...The end is the means...When you perceive for yourself that violence only leads to greater harm, is it difficult to drop violence?

J. Krishnamurti
Commentaries on Living
Third Series

— • —

We seek the freedom of free men, and the construction of a world where Martin Luther King could have lived and preached non-violence.

Nikki Giovanni
The Funeral of
Martin Luther King, Jr.

— • —

CHAPTER THREE
Desire And Longing

Reflective people have observed in themselves times when they are full of nameless longings, a kind of welling up of deep springs of sadness, a feeling of grief that seems to cling and linger. These longings sometimes suggest restlessness without discernible destination, an unexplainable dissatisfaction, a moodiness without a cause. You can sometimes spot such times in people when their eyes seem to roam the heavens or the ceilings of the rooms they inhabit as if answers might be forthcoming. Children wait for Christmas, saints wait for visions. What are we waiting for?

Sometimes, desire is more specific. Wanting something, someplace, someone is the more usual and greater problem for most of us.

Desire can be sexual. Sexual desire in our complex society has become equally complex. It is no longer simply an animalistic heat or nature's push to reproduce. It isn't even as simple as a demonstration of affection or passion between one human being and another. Sexual desire has become one of our measurements, our competitions: How much do I feel? How much is felt for me? How can I get more of it to prove I am still young and desirable and important to somebody?

Desire can be for more food, a warmer house — among those whose lives are ravaged by persecution, starvation, homelessness, any food, any warmth, any shelter. And as with sexual desire, the desire for special food and finer shelter has graduated from basic and natural need to a measure of our success and importance. Desire can be for company among the lonely, clarity among the confused and mentally ill, the chemically imbalanced. Again, these desires are life wanting to live itself as our bodies are cells wanting to replicate in order to survive — until even these desires graduate from a little needed company to proof of social position, from a need for clarity into a need for sainthood.

The desire that plagues us psychologically is something different surely than simple need. For most of us, whatever form desire takes, it is based on society telling us that whatever we are, we are not enough. Always to live in a state of becoming something more, or something else, or something better is what produces that continual state of being uncomfortable in the skin. The desire can be for more sex with more people for becoming more desirable with every passing year. The desire can be for power, money, possessions, security, comfort, to be loved, for permanent life, for immortality in the next life, for fame in this one. (The latter is my personal burr under the psychological saddle.)

Desire itself is natural, delightful, stimulating. Without desire, you would be dead. People who desire, who have an appetite for life, who have an interesting taste or passion, are marvelous to be around. Unfortunately, we've been told by too many religions in too many cultures that desire, sexual, psychological, or otherwise, is wrong to feel. This makes no sense. If you are alive, you want.

The problem is not desire itself. The problem is when thought steps in the moment you feel a desire, and says, "Desire must be fulfilled. You must have what you want." We are never taught psychological desire will pass whether it is satisfied or not, and simply fix itself to the next thing. We are never told we don't have to have the thing we want, that we won't die of longing, that our attention ought to be on why we have been told we're not enough and we need something out there to make us enough.

It is not desire itself that is the problem. The problem with desire is when it gets out of hand, out of control, or in your way so it interferes with someone else's life, or your own life, or leaves you in a state of obsession, or deprived depression. The problem with the human brain is that we don't seem to be able to treat desire simply and appropriately like other animals. There is nothing wrong with wanting a new car or a new suit of clothes if your life requires them, or you simply enjoy something and your pocketbook can afford them. Why do we make a problem? What is desire?

If you watch it rise up inside you, you can see that desire comes from our senses, with thought added like cayenne pepper. You see a jacket you like, a nice jacket. You notice in a store or on someone else's back. Then you begin to think: that jacket would look nice on me. I want it for myself. I desire it. Or you meet a man or woman at the office, at a party. You admire the face, the body, the smile, the hair. You think, what a marvelous person, right size and shape, would look nice on me. You admire the owner of a yacht, a corporation, a small country, or the writer of a bestseller or a movie star, and you think, money and power and fame are really nice. It would be nice for me, all that power and admiration and attention.

It is one of the hardest things to see that just because you want something, this doesn't mean you have to have it. You could see it, admire it, leave it where you found it. It's the longing for things that causes the problem, not admiration, desire, or even need. It is neither sin, mistake, nor problem just to admire and enjoy the sight of something, the experience of it, the company of someone. We have developed a cultural habit of experiencing something pleasurable: a perfect summer evening, full moon, lovely music; a crisp, fall day at a football game; an elegant dinner; good sex; a flowering garden; the beach at sunset; or even a moment of uninvited joy — and we think, I must have that again, I must have more, I must find a way to hang on to it, buy it, preserve it, repeat it often in the future. The next repetition of the experience may only be mechanical pleasure rather than a newly unfolding joy. Joy is a gift. It can't be repeated by arranging for it, as you well know if you have ever tried to repeat a perfect moment or experience.

It is worth inquiring into the cause of all this excessive wanting of pleasure. The cause may well be misery: the misery of repetitive living without thinking through what it is you want, instead of what you've been told to want. It may be the misery of hating your work, having no job at all, hating your life, hardly living at all. An overload of desire only tells you the rest of your life is miserable, or empty of meaning, that your life lacks joy and creativity and affection and enthusiasm. It does not seem necessary to suggest that no new jacket in the world or even a new motorcycle is going to fix all that.

Whenever, therefore, you feel as if you are obsessing over something at your car dealer, at the mall, in your neighbor's bed, whenever you want something or someone inappropriate or too much, examine the rest of your life and find a way to live it better. If your own life feels good to you, if it is rich and full, if it goes up and down and up again and you are able to sustain the duller periods we all go through because your life is basically the way you want it, you won't need to fix it with something or someone else. Feeling good physically comes from exercising all the body muscles, back, arms, legs, heart, lungs. Feeling good psychologically, emotionally and intellectually, is the same. To love and sorrow, work, play, give, take, sleep — not to use yourself up brings depression, ache, longing. It isn't necessary to take anyone else's word for this. You can experiment with all this for yourself.

You can try these practices to quiet both body and brain for meditation.

Salute the Sun

1. Stand tall, body weight evenly distributed, rib cage lifted up out of pelvis, stomach and butt tucked in. Bring fingers and palms together over heart. Breathe deeply and slowly through exercise.

(1)

(2)   (3)

2. Raise arms, bend slightly back to stretch front of body, tighten buttocks to protect lower back.

3. Bend forward, hanging from hips, legs as straight as possible, hands on mat on either side of feet.

4. Head up, hands on floor, stretch right foot back, then left foot, keeping your body level, slanted like a slide.

(4a)   (4b)

(5a)   (5b)

5. Lower knees, chest, chin to floor, then slowly, carefully arch your back into cobra position.

6. Point toes forward, push with your hands to help you raise your hips until your body is a V, hang head, lower heels to floor for calf stretch.

7. Step between your hands with left foot, then right. Hang from hips, head and arms relaxed and loose.

(6)   (7)

(7a)　　　　　　　　(8)

8. Inhale, come up slowly breathing out, feeling every vertebrae uncoil, until you are standing.

9. Bend back slowly, come forward, bring hands into greet-
   ing position.

(9a)　　　　　　　　(9b)

Sitting Meditation

Try a sitting meditation while focusing on a candle.

Sit in your usual comfortable, quiet place. This time, place a lighted candle three feet in front of you on the floor or low table. Sit in your meditation posture. Gaze at the flame for two minutes. Close your eyes and press your palms gently against your closed lids. You will see the image of the flame. Concentrate, don't wander from the image for a minute or so. Rest in your meditation posture quietly and follow your thoughts for five minutes, dropping the words desire and longing into your silence.

Discover what you want, know your self's desires. Enjoy the delight they give you: note any urgency to satisfy and the engendered distress. Some of your desires you can work for, if they are appropriate and unharmful to yourself or anyone else. Some you may decide to relinquish because you see through them. In either case, don't waste your energy in longings. And don't just settle for enjoying one small corner of life: enjoy the whole spectacle, the entire glorious show.

— • —

That thou mayest have pleasure in everything, seek pleasure in nothing...That thou mayest possess all things, seek to possess nothing...That thou mayest be everything, seek to be nothing.

St. John of the Cross
The Ascent of Mount Carmel

— • —

— • —

These desires, — for the sex relation, for material and emotional security, and for companionship — are perfectly necessary and right, and surely God-given. Self run riot is the problem.

Bill Wilson
Founder of Alcoholics Anonymous
Twelve Steps and Twelve Traditions

— • —

CHAPTER FOUR
Relationship And Isolation:
How To Live In This World Without Damage

It isn't necessary in this world, unless you are stranded on a Mongolian steppe or an Alaskan glacier, to be lonely. There are six billion of us, most of us huddled together in bunches, in families, communities, towns, and cities, on this planet. While it's true 85% of all life turns out to be bacteria, we are larger and particularly visible, especially to each other.

Yet strangely, we live and feel as if we were often entirely unable to touch another human being. We live internally isolated, we feel lonely. Sometimes, it can seem as if there were a dark well under the feet where firm ground ought to be. It is especially confusing when the tricky sensation of isolation occurs when you are among friends, in the night lying right next to your husband or wife, in the middle of Christmas dinner with your family, and where there ought to be close warmth and connection, there is a swift, sudden awareness of being alone, out of touch and tune, a solitary figure at the rim of the universe. I mean, everybody is right there! So why does it feel so lonely?

Since all life is relationship, why is it such a perennial struggle instead of as natural as breathing in a sunlit afternoon? Everything is relationship. There is not only relationship between people, but between each of us and the very oxygen we take into our systems as we breathe, the sunlight and the chemistry of our brains, the parents we came from, the children we bear, the chairs we sit on, the clothes, cars, houses we inhabit, the food, sounds, sights, textures, and smells that affect our systems. We have a relationship to our society's images: of money (how much is necessary to be respected); age (how young you have to be to be to be loved and desired); health (how fit on a scale of one to ten to avoid being called a has-been). These personal and sociological and biological relationships are not all. We are also related to the cosmos. Gravity, magnetic fields, the space-time continuum of the universe — we are in relationship to it all. With most of these, our cognitive capacity, thought, can analyze relationship, can establish connection.

But something happens, something gets in the way and causes problems in our relationship with one another. Why do we have so many problems with each other? Is it because, out of fear and confusions, we have formed so many bad habits psychologically and one of these habits is that we use instead of love one another?

There are many passages in our lives when this habit is more evident than at other times, when there seems to be a kind of desperation in our relationships. In childhood, it is normal that we depend for everything on others. In our teens, we have one foot in our parents' homes, and with the other we test the waters of the pools of the world, half still dependent, half on our way out. Teens are a lonely time, when you don't really belong in your parents' home any more, but you haven't yet gotten ready to make a home of your own. Not only biology, but our culture tells us mating is the answer, if you could at least just have someone to love and to love you, someone who belonged to you, someone to keep you strong, the two of you would be safe together, shoulder to shoulder facing the big, outer world. The trouble is, it doesn't work. In a world built only for two, you end by eating each other alive.

It doesn't take a rocket scientist to figure out what goes wrong here. Deeply pondered life experience is all that is needed. Obviously, mating is natural. Life wants life, to reproduce itself. But in our fear of loneliness, in our confusion about why humans are even here facing the vast dark unknown of the universe, in our terror of our own perceptions of death, we expect, and we are encouraged by our own myths and commercials to hope for more from the intimate relationship with one other person than it can possibly provide. This is only a bad habit, this hopeful expectation, and observation, insight, can correct it.

There are other passages in our lives that may illustrate how we deal with one another through images. In mid-life, many need reassurance that they are still young and desirable; it is difficult to outgrow youth, the feeling of being forever physically and mentally invincible, the dream of financial success, or an island where perfect happiness is possible. We look at each other during this passage with more than usual need for psychological help rather than affection — and therefore, at least in our country, divorce, mental illnesses like depression and alcoholism or other addictions rise.

There are many life passages, but the next most evident one in our country (in other countries, the older people are either dead or better taken care of as well as, in some cultures, actually honored for their years if not their wisdom) is the passage into our sixties, seventies, and eighties. Life in these decades, known variously as senior years, golden years, elder citizenry, are made possible by medical advances, better nutrition, Social Security and Medicare, retirement plans, assisted living services and communities, and so forth. But there is still the problem of image, the habits of thought. And sometimes the most subtle and difficult relationships one can have are to society's images, the ones we all carry in our brains, of money, of age, of health, of growing older, poorer, less physically able. Personally, I have just lived through the week from hell. I was informed that my income was down because of interest rates (and likely to remain so), my blood pressure and cholesterol levels were up (and without fistfuls of pills were likely to remain so), and I had reached the age, according to my oldest and dear friend Claire when the time had come to apply for Social Security benefits. Since I am already on Prozac for mild depression, there was nothing to do but observe, meditate, ponder over my relationships to my brain's images. Two weeks ago, I felt like a healthy, productive, energetic, moderately successful writer and publisher, an active and attractive if slightly (and becomingly, I am told) silvering mother and grandmother, a world traveler, wildlife rehabilitator, a generally serviceable human being. Now, overnight, I am griefstricken, this clearly being the what the sudden downer was about. I am exactly the same person, but like everyone else I have images in my brain, and through my relationship to those images, instead of a vigorous woman in her prime with friends, family, and a satisfying if not always remunerative profession, I now see a poor, old lady living on cat food, puttering about, doddering down a dimming lonely path of helpless days, dwindling years.

It was all, as they say, with perfect accuracy, in the mind. My life was, is, fine. All that had changed was my relationship to society's images, the ones lodged in my brain. To see that, even for a moment, was extraordinary. The insight has changed the neurochemistry in my brain, so that each day I feel better. Mental illness is, after all, neurochemistry gone wrong. Mental health is the brain's neurochemistry righting itself constantly. Insight, the insight that changes attitude toward relationship, is the factor of that change. (Insight, incidentally, may also include reaching for the help of pharmacology, if and when necessary.)

Images are a large part of our difficulties in relationship to ourselves. In the same way, words and images are a large part of our problems with each other, with all human relationships. Instead of seeing another person directly (you can experiment with this yourself), if you hang a word — like those wordcards in school — with its image of husband/wife, parent/child, boss/employee, woman/man, boyfriend/girlfriend, on someone, you suddenly have ideas, preconceptions, and expectations of how the other person is supposed to behave. Try this out for a day, if you're interested to experiment. Label the people you come into contact with in your daily life, and you'll see how fixed are your expectations of them, how a wife is supposed to behave, or a husband, a son, a daughter, a friend. Just hang a name or label on someone

and watch your reactions. Even your own behavior changes when you label or name a role for someone else. A once loving parent and child suddenly behave like royalty and rebel. A once independent female behaves as if her spine had turned to worms; a once pleasant man, given authority with the word 'boss' acts like Attila the Hun.

Human relationship is an excellent and most valuable mirror in which to see yourself and your behavior. You can see yourself, in the way you relate to and behave with your friends and family, your lover, your work, your own angers and insecurities, your own neediness, competitive rages, your own moments of generosity, kindness, helpfulness. You can see everything you are in a few hours, just paying attention to your interactions. It is positively fascinating the way the words and images invented in thought affect us so much more than what's really going on.

You might also try going somewhere and looking at your relationship to nature. If you live in a city, look at a pigeon or a sparrow or a squirrel. If you are blessed with living in the countryside, there is a greater variety of wildlife. Do you have an image of them as annoyances? Are you afraid of them coming too close? Do you see them simply as other nations occupying different spaces next to you, with their own rights and ways of life, children and homes to care for? Do you see the cosmic picture, that we are all on the same planet, that we will all go out together when the sun burns out, plant, and animal, including us? Or do you entertain the common cultural image that humans are somehow superior, entitled to dominate? Look at your relationship to the clouds, the trees, marshes, and meadows, city parks full of millions of creatures, beings living their lives in the here and how — all this truth of life just living itself knocks against our heads and what do we say? "I have to conquer it to understand," or "Leave me alone, I'm searching for the truth through science and books." And so, one more time, it all moves back and away. Our brains are so busy telling us what we like and what we don't like, what we think we need and what we think we do not need, we're so full of ideas and opinions about everything, we miss our whole relationship to everything around us, and the fact that our atoms are part of all the other atoms, and our isolation and loneliness are only words and an attitude after all.

David Bohm, the great theoretical physicist and friend of Einstein's, proposed that:

— • —

What we call empty space contains an immense background of energy (ed. note: more energy than can be accounted for by measuring matter), and that matter, as we know it is a small, 'quantized' wavelike excitation on top of this background, like a tiny ripple on a vast sea...empty space is actually...the ground for the existence of everything, including ourselves.

David Bohm
Wholeness and the Implicate Order

— • —

Further, Bohm sees no particle of difference between animate and inanimate matter: a molecule of carbon dioxide that crosses a cell boundary into a leaf does not suddenly 'come alive' nor does a molecule of oxygen die when released into the air, then come alive again when human beings breathe it in. Rather, he says, "life itself has to be regarded as belonging...to a totality, including plants, us, and environment." There is no fundamental difference between us, and no fundamental difference between us and a rock on a mountain, it seems.

Seems everything is holy, or nothing is at all.

You can deepen the ocean of your consciousness with attention to what is true. As the great writer Somerset Maugham once said, and I'm quoting very roughly, "Before you get smart, you think you're a separate drop of water in the ocean. When you get smarter, you decide to join the rest of the drops of water in the ocean. Real intelligence is to see you've been part of the ocean all along."

What is love then, we must ask?

As you look at yourself and understand yourself in relationship, and the way words, images, thought get in the way of actual relationship, it is easier to see what love is not.

- Love is not the temporary seductiveness of two people living under a quilt (in an illusion of safety) in the damp, claustrophobic coziness of a cave.

- Love is not clutching at another person for dear life to keep you alive (think of life-saving techniques in deep waters: a stranglehold around the rescuer's neck and you both go under).

- Love is not dependency: if you watch, you will see dependency creates mostly fear of losing what you depend on, and anger that nobody lives up to what you think you need (obviously it's good to have companionship, affection, sharing love and life together, but this is not the same as fighting for lap space — you both end up on the floor that way).

- Love is not, contrary to popular songs, using each other for sustenance — only vampire bats and mosquitoes suck another's blood.

- Love is not jealousy, control, possession (this does not advocate sexual and emotional promiscuity; freedom does not mean doing whatever you like).

- Love is not a mood, or a sentiment, a feeling you happen to have at the moment.

Love loves. Not just for a return on investment, but because love is simply a state of being without any actual object. It's a state of communion, connection, affection, with no goals, no ulterior motives, no self. Where the self is, love is not; when the self comes into it, love goes out of it.

Facing ourselves in this business of what we have always called loving and relationship requires humor, demands honesty, and will most certainly need courage to face down the embarrassment (at least, most of us will be embarrassed) at discovering how needy, possessive, obsessive, angry, controlling, manipulating, and generally unattractive we are in relationship to other people, as well as in relationship to institutions like money, marriage, community, work.

Before you face your various selves, don't forget that some facets of you will turn out to be lovely, loving, generous, kindly. This is not an ordeal of self-hate, only of understanding your self from moment to changing moment throughout your day and your life.

You might try a relaxation exercise to begin with.

1. Lie flat on floor or bed.

2. Tense every muscle group one after the other, beginning with toes, feet, legs, buttocks, and up the back to shoulders, arms, fists, then up the neck to the face, squeezing the face together like a prune.

3. Take a deep breath. Let go suddenly, all the muscles and the breath.

4. Now relax all the muscles in the same order. With attention, relax every muscle group one after the other, toes,
   feet, legs, buttocks, back, arms, hands, neck, head, face.

5. Do five deep meditation breaths, slowly filling the belly
   for a count of five, push air up into lungs, hold for ten,
   breathe slowly out for ten.

Now do your sitting. Into your silence drop the words 'lone-liness,' then 'relationship.' Even in only five or ten minutes of sitting, especially if you can watch, not argue with yourself, not judge yourself, just look, you can learn a great deal about yourself and the ways in which you relate to people and the life you live, to your work, to money, to the religious, national, community groups to which you are attached.

— • —

Avoid becoming a mirror image of those men who value power above life, and control over love.

Maya Angelou
Wouldn't Take Nothing
For My Journey Now

— • —

There is a common need to escape, and mutually we use each other. This usage is called love. You do not like what you are, and so you run away from yourself.

J. Krishnamurti
Total Freedom

— • —

— • —

Thus it seems that inner and outer work are two sides of the same undertaking. The inner work we do to become more wakeful and present can only benefit our relations with others, just as our relationships cannot help but show us where we have more work to do on ourselves.

John Welwood
Ordinary Magic:
Everyday Life As Spiritual Path

— • —

CHAPTER FIVE
Sex And Marriage

Sex is so natural, so necessary for the reproduction of life, so satisfying in its sensations, so prevalent throughout the entire range of living nations, tribes, and kingdoms, the question that must be asked is: Why do human beings alone make such a problem of it? Why are we so preoccupied with something as natural as eating or breathing, as biologically necessary for the reproduction of life. Sex is pleasurable, available even to the poorest among us, and physically common to all human beings. Yet we continue to make sex a psychological preoccupation: we think about sex so much of the time. We even think sex is the only way to make love.

To understand the problem of sex, therefore, it is necessary to understand the brain that makes a problem out of sex in the first place. In our species, instead of functioning with a wholeness of purpose, our brains function in fragments, one self or image or idea or pleasure always fighting the other, dividing up into choruses of arguing voices. The voices take up the various parts that reflect the teachings of some rigid religions and their traditions which say sex is bad. This voice is so strong in some people that they decide that celibacy is a virtue or the way to heaven. It is possible to waste a good deal of energy repressing one of nature's most pressing functions.

The magazines, self-help books, television programs, and movies running through your head say sex is good, and the more sex you have, the sexier you are. American culture even suggests that along with money and winning, sex is a way to measure how terrific you are. It is possible also, and just as silly, to waste a good deal of energy proving that nature's need is your own personal, talented victory.

It is not sex that corrupts, it's our preoccupation with sex. Reflecting the voices of some religions, many parents, in order to ensure that there will be no unwanted offspring, no scandal, have said the same thing: repress your sexual needs. But it isn't religions and parents that make the problem go on: it is us, because we carry on listening to those voices in our heads and even pass them on to our children. But what is the point of wasting energy and time denying sex? Until the sun burns out, sex is clearly here to stay: for the joy of it; to give us our children; for connection to another human being; because it gives us the few precious moments in our lifetimes when we truly can forget, get out of ourselves and our problems; and it gives those of us who hunger for complete attention a few moments of the utter, absorbed attention of another human being.

Believe it or not, it doesn't, in the long run, or even the short, make any difference at all to the fate of the universe whether you go to bed with someone or not. It is not sex that's the difficulty. It is our misuse of sex: refusal to be responsible if there is a child or to use prevention in the first place; the inappropriate choice of sex partner (someone else's mate, someone too old or too young), the use of sex for the wrong reasons — to gain power, to give pain. And the voices in our heads that produce guilt, blame, all inherited from tribal patterns thousands of years ago when inclusion or exclusion from tribal social usage meant literal life or death.

It is constant preoccupation and inappropriate motive that are the problems, not sex itself. Once again, thought has entered into a human activity, instead of intelligence and affection, to distort our behavior. What ought to be a simple and natural connection between two people has been corrupted by the contents of thoughts and their intrusion into an area of our lives where thought does not belong. This does not mean the opposite, that you run around in thoughtless promiscuity whenever the mood strikes. Obsessive preoccupation is neither healthy nor appropriate. We need to understand the natural instincts to eat, have a home, and have sex, not stuff ourselves to capacity, grab everything in sight for ourselves, and copulate with impunity. Obsession with any corner, any fragment of one's life, obviously affects all the other parts of one's life as well. So if there is disorder in my sex life, my work life, my relationship to my children, all other relationships will be distorted, badly affected.

The question is then, why do we think otherwise? What makes us suppose we can have disorder in that most intimate connection, our roiling preoccupation with sex (this is true whether we are having any or not), and it simply won't affect the rest of our lives — when it's clear that disorder in any area affects all the other areas. It just isn't possible to be a slave to some pleasurable fragment, to be locked into one small room of the brain, and live a full life. Personally, I don't like slavery. Not even to myself — or any one of my selves.

Being able to see this constant fragmentation in thought in our most intimate lives is very freeing. It helps, if the understanding is very deep and not just an academic or superficial exercise, to change one's behavior over sexual or any other preoccupation. In the changing of behavior, in the very questioning of things one never questioned before, the neurons of the brain, the chemistry of the brain actually, physically changes. This understanding of our slavery is the key to freedom — if, of course, one is interested in freedom from the human tendency, genetically and physically based the molecular biologists now tell us, toward violence, addiction, and emotional pain. Remembering that the power of money and sex are frequently at the base of all three, we can change not only our own fates, but those of our generations to come, in altering our mental chemistry now. It is exciting, when you think about it — the fact that it is not only possible to alter one's own neurochemistry, to mutate, that is, but in so doing, to alter the course of human history. (The influence of and for the good of the human race by one individual can be just as powerful as the evil, fear, suffering one person like Hitler caused generations of the human race.) Freedom from emotional pain has as powerful an effect as causing it. This is not sentiment: this is molecular fact. Our brains are physical material.

Take the cortex, for example, of the human brain. The cortex simply means the outer layer of an organ. The temporal cortex, the outer layer of the brain behind the temples, seems to be where memories of the past may be evoked by electrical stimulation. Behind our right ear is a pea-sized area of the brain that primates (humans, monkeys and our cousin apes orangutans, gorillas, chimpanzees and bonobos) use for face-watching — to assess one another's moods, feelings, acceptance, rejection. It is a shock some-

times to discover how actual, how physically actual, thinking and feeling are. And therefore perfectly possible to alter, to change. This means we can all (as we all share the same brain) really see the truth of something and change ourselves, so that we stop doing what hurts us and others in our marriages, in our love affairs, in our own sex lives and the attitudes about sex or any facet of our lives we pass on to our children. What we are talking about isn't just a good idea: it is entirely possible to do. Why we don't do it, is only because most people don't take the meditative time to see that we can. You can't legislate change. You can only change.

This leads to the interesting subject of marriage, why it is so often lonely, sometimes unsatisfying, occasionally disappointing, and, in our country, increasingly a failure. After the first flush of victory and pleasure, something happens, and instead of growing deeper, more companionable, more loving, marriage often simply covers like a pretty but suffocating quilt two isolated people. The problems in marriage relationships may be based on our reasons for marrying in the first place. Why do we marry? Or not marry?

This is an excellent meditation for anyone over the age of puberty. While nature has a natural urge to replicate itself, society creates much pressure over natural behavior. To keep its women safe from sexual predation, to safeguard property values, to contain disease, to curb population, our culture prefers men and women to live in contained couples, to live in ongoing relationship with a single partner. This cultural curb can create disturbances in many people's sexual inclinations.

Sit and let the disturbance happen in your mind. It is always easier, of course to do your sitting when all is going well for you and your thoughts are pleasant. It is much harder to sit when the emotional sky is gray with depression or stormy with emotional disturbance. Sometimes, it is in exactly this state that centering yourself in sitting meditation can do you the most good. Patience is the ability not to resist: noise, irritation, frustration, inconvenience. Instead of the gritted teeth of forbearance, sit patiently with yourself, realizing that it may not work at first, that it may not work all the time, that there may be days when it will not work at all. Give it up if you feel you can't face the particular subject of marriage on this particular day, and try again later.

I once asked a friend what his definition of meditation was in the face of a sudden fear or anger or ongoing resentment. He was quiet a moment. Then he said two words.

— • —

Stand back.

Mark Kaufman
Teacher and Director
United Taikwondo Training Center

— • —

So, sit down, if you will, stand back, and ask yourself: why did I marry or choose to live with this partner?

- Because I was lonely, my life was bleak and empty before I found this person.

- This person filled my life, provided safe haven, a center to revolve around, gave my life a structure, kept me too busy to think about being lonely.

- Because everybody else was getting married, was married or living in couples, and I felt left out of the social pattern.

- My church, temple, religion, community, my mother, told me to.

- To keep out the cold.

- For sex, money, for children.

- For general security from the seen and unseen vicissitudes of the world.

- For companionship now and in my old age, to have a personal hostage to stand by me and comfort me throughout the ages and stages of life.

- A mystical, uncontrollable sense of destiny that this one person was THE ONE.

- Couldn't help it — I was pregnant, broke, out of a job, out of a house, out of my mind, and marriage seemed to be the solution.

- Feeling different and left out, marriage seemed to include me in the river of human activity around me.

- For the sense of family, for the sense of having someone to look after me, take care of me, tell me what to do.

- For approval, a support system, someone in my corner, behind me, for me.

These are many of the thoughts and feelings people experience when they meditate on marriage. You will, if you don't resist what you hear in your brain, discover exactly your own reasons for marriage, or without a piece of paper, your reasons for living with people and not getting married.

For now, only reflect that there is no right or wrong here, just the seeing of what goes on for you.

Technically, the origin of marriage was to establish ownership of the woman, to ensure legal protection for a man and wife and their legally appropriate children for inheritance purposes. Marriage was sanctioned for the safety both of the two people involved, and for the children. Even fidelity was based on property rights, so that the woman behaved herself, and so that out-of-the-family children did not inherit. Eventually, the sacrament of marriage included the spiritual and psychological and emotionally aspects of life: a vow between two people to care for one another and their children.

In very recent times, as the history of the human race goes, marriage got confused with romance, sexual pleasure, and the general chaos of unmatured psychological needs, particularly the need to escape the loneliness caused by not understanding what our own feeling of emptiness is all about — not a lack of love, but a lack of loving!

— • —

The loneliness, bleakness, wretchedness you feel without this per-
son you love by your side existed before you fell in love. What you
call love is merely stimulation, the temporary covering-up of your
emptiness. You escaped from loneliness though a person, used this
person to cover it up. Your problem is not this relationship...it is
the problem of your own emptiness. Escape is very dangerous be-
cause, like some drug, it hides the real problem. It is because you
have no love inside you that you continually look for love to fill
you from the outside. This lack of love is your loneliness, and
when you see the truth of this you will never again try to fill it
with things and people from outside...

There is a difference between understanding the futility of this
escape and deciding not to get involved in...relationship...It is
going beyond feeling and thinking, sidestepping them. Whatever
is happening inside you — anger, depression, jealousy or any other
conflict at all — drop it instantly. Stop it.

J. Krishnamurti
Meeting Life

— • —

Marriage is simply the legal decision of two people to un-
dertake an emotional and physical decision to join their
lives: for children and their protection; for companionship; for a
joint journey through their lives. The complications, as always,
are in relationship. Since relationship is not possession, not colo-
nizing another human being for purposes of economic, emotional,
psychological, parental, physical support (which does not mean
we should not take care of one another in whatever way each fam-

ily deems appropriate), can we possibly live together without interior conflict or ulterior motive? That is, without the attachment, the dependency that have their evolutionary roots in the long, helpless childhoods of our species. We do not need, as adults, to go on believing that if we are abandoned by another, we will die. It is the fear, often, of impermanence that holds us back from intimacy, when obviously transiency must be embraced for intimacy to be possible. What we call sanity and harmony is perhaps simply the ability to let intimate moments come and go in our relationships. We all want sane relationships; but we have to have sanity ourselves to recognize sanity in others when it comes along.

Why is it we all want so desperately to be loved? Because we are all so desperately empty of love and therefore lonely.

If we can watch self as a movement of thought come in to everything, not only in sitting meditation, but in daily life, in all relationships, and if we can recognize it each time it comes up and defuse it, we stand a chance at connecting with each other and ending loneliness inside marriage and out.

Observing, watching yourself in this way, being aware when self intrudes where it ought not to in the middle of relationship, will bring you all the clarity required. Paying attention is far more effective than trying to remember rules, following the prescriptions for marriage, friendship, parenthood issued rapid fire from every pulpit and podium. Memory, whether your own or collective, has no place in love.

CHAPTER SIX
Work And Ambition

Many people think of work and ambition, the way they think of sports and competition, as synonymous. We are all educated in school to meet society's demands, particularly in Western culture and most particularly in the United States of America. We are expected to meet them, not necessarily with honor, fairness, and kindness to all, but with as much power, money, and disregard for the means as possible as long as the ends are met. Americans, as a relatively new culture on the planet comprised of people from every nationality, every major religion, most ethnic groups, many tribes, are evidence of what is happening everywhere: there may have been physical evolution; there has been no psychological or behavioral evolution at all.

Carolus Linnaeus, the great eighteenth-century Swedish naturalist, created the system of biological classification we continue to use to this day. He arranged plants and animals in groups that resembled each other in a hierarchy of complexity. Our species he named homo sapiens — 'wise person ' — and put us, along with monkeys and apes, in the order primates. Primates include two families. There are the hominidae (ourselves and our immediate ancestors) and the pongidae (orangutans, gorillas, chimpanzees, their pigmy cousins the bonobos). Linnaeus understood and identified the patterns of relationships among all forms of life. He recognized the similarities between humans and apes. But it was Charles Darwin, in his *On the Origin of Species by Means of Natural Selection* (1859) who explained physical evolution. Plants and animals produce more offspring than the planet can support. This creates constant competition for physical survival. Some offspring are taller or shorter, more agile, more camouflaged, whatever it takes to better adapt to their environment. These attract the best mates, produce more surviving offspring who inherit the adaptive traits, and the offspring pass these traits on into a continually

physically evolving population. Physical evolution includes the brain and its size and functions as well bones, muscle, teeth, hair, skin, heartbeat.

In one sense, therefore, we are what we are, physically: chimpanzees occasionally cannabalize each other's babies — we bomb each other's babies; orangutans force reproductive sex on their females — we have been known to rape our women during wars and raids, to say nothing of in the streets and the marital beds; gorillas are pretty gentle, but the men fool around a lot with as many women as they can. And all primates take as much territory, fruit, and nuts from the next foraging group as they can.

We are primates of the animal kingdom just like the rest of the primates. But we are also the self-aware, the thinking primate. This ability to think, however, as we have been discovering in this book, may have its drawbacks. So far, what thinking has led to is images of ourselves as bigger, better, more. Because of our larger, more complex brains and opposable thumbs, we have been able to invent the tools, laboratories, and weapons to implement those images, until we have turned ourselves into bigger bullies, better at causing ourselves and each other pain, and made ourselves more unhappy than ever. As Stephen Jay Gould keeps reminding us, we are a twig in the tree of life, not the star at the top of the tree: we have not yet worked out our kinks.

What we are further, however, is the reflective primate. We have receptors for intelligence, a sense of the greater mystery of life, god, the universe, that sense of exaltation and wonder, unmotivated passion that is truly love, the profound sense of connection with all things that is the true foundation of science and religion.

Since our species homo sapiens has proved capable of the highest, most complex physical evolution this planet has experienced in its four and a half billion years, and since we are also capable of going beyond the merely physical capacity to be the most ruthless, aggressive, vicious of all animals ever — why don't we do it?

Why don't we learn for ourselves and be an example for our children that the demands of society are simply an outward expression of all of our inner selves, and if we are greedy, envious, aggressive inwardly, all society will be likewise?

Why don't we learn and teach our children about good, satisfying work that hurts no one else, that does not corrupt the environment, that does not consume us with personal ambition, that leaves enough personal leisure time to actually live one's life instead of watch it rush by?

Why don't we learn and teach our children that there will always be someone richer, more powerful, more famous — and that to spend your life force killing and being killed in one competition after another especially on a planet where, at least for our species, there is truly enough to go around or an inventable way to make sure of it...is to waste a life?

Webster's Dictionary defines ambition as a desire for rank, fame, or power. Unless one is running scared, why does one need rank, fame, or power?

This is an increasingly expensive world to live in. It is more difficult than ever, requires more education and information and sophisticated communications skills to live in. Most of us are urban or suburban, with little interest in farming or pioneering, and even those endeavors have become rather more technical than they once were. We are not dependent children, we must have money to live on, and to earn money these days requires complex skills, education, even pieces of paper that prove we have learned something. There is not the slightest suggestion in these pages that we all stop in our tracks and go on the dole or try to squeeze back into the parental womb.

But it doesn't have to mean the opposite, that we rape each other and pillage the earth on the way to the top of the landfill heap or any other heap, and label and pass on to our children this horrendous activity as 'worthy ambition.' This phrase may have to be stuffed in the shredder along with 'making war for peace,' or 'this beating hurts me more than it hurts you,' or 'crime doesn't pay,' and other laughable classics.

This is such a troublesome meditation, how to live in this world and pay one's way with the right ways and means of livelihood as a true homo sapiens, that a walking meditation might work better than a sitting meditation, if only to connect you with the larger life of the wind in the trees, the movement of light on water, other people on the city pavements, the dust under your feet. Questions to consider as you walk:

- How do you feel about the work you do? Do you love it, like it, tolerate it, hate it?

- Do you think of your work as generally helpful to the state of humanity, as a contribution, as a ladder to personal importance, to money, position, power?

- Given a choice, would you change your work? If so, to what?

- If in your meditation you decide your work harms rather than helps humanity, are you capable of changing?

- Would you have made different choices? And if the answer is yes, why don't you change now?

My favorite mantra on walking meditations is:

It isn't all about me. When I count myself, I'm not so many.

Zen masters say:

All work is equally important.

The Bible says:

Man shall not live by bread alone.

Shakespeare says, in *The Tempest*:

The cloud-capped towers, the gorgeous palaces,
The solemn temples, the great globe itself,
…shall dissolve…
We are such stuff
As dreams are made on, and our little life
Is rounded with a sleep.

Coming and going, we are children of the universe, each equally important and only important as we affect everything else. We each can, and must, live up to this, or go down in flames together. Perhaps nothing more than the way we choose whether to compete or to cooperate in our work will affect the outcome.

CHAPTER SEVEN
Self-Awareness,
Self-Knowledge, The Keys
To Freedom And Power

Personally, I like to take my shower by myself. I prefer, when I look in the bathroom mirror, to see reflected only my face. I do not like looking into a trick mirror that turns only me into receding casts of thousands extending back into the generational mists of time.

The difficulty is, there are still times when the bathtub under the shower faucet, and the mirror as I brush my teeth are so crowded with all the people in my head, talking, shouting, yelling at me, commenting on my appearance, my performance, my bank account, the way I've raised my children, the work I do, the food I cook, the way I keep house, my general failure to live up to expectation, never mind raising the bar a fraction of an inch, or in any way return the investment made in me by my hardworking forebears, that I want to hang myself from the towel rack until either 1) I stop breathing, or 2) they stop yelling at me, whichever happens first.

Sadly, all of us know the feeling. All you're doing is washing under your arms or shaving some socially required section of your face or body, and your brain starts imaging your mother, your father, your boss, your friends, coworkers, children, bowling league, poker game buddies, all having the opinions about you that you have imagined in your worst nightmares.

To make it worse, to increase the decibel level until your bathroom has become the inside of a dozen speakers, you begin to answer all of them back.

This happens to me also at four o'clock in the morning, after too much dinner coffee, in bed. There arise from all the shadowy corners of the room, there issue from under the sheets, from darkened closets, from beneath the bed, there emanate from the very walls to whisper and echo, all those voices to repeat exactly what they told me earlier in the bathroom.

It happens in the car. It can happen in that dead time around three o'clock in the afternoon when I stare unfocused past the computer out of the window at the marsh and sky. It is what prevents me from running away up a high mountain to escape civilization and sit like the holy man in Rumer Godden's *Black Narcissus* and spend the rest of my life contemplating glorious sunsets in miraculous skies.

What I am afraid of, what I know perfectly well will happen, is that all those voices will follow me because they are all inside my head. (If you don't have this problem, you are a rare human being. If you have the answer as to why they can never, never find anything nice to say, call or write.)

Part of the trouble with all those voices is that you begin to supply them with a judge, jury, prosecutor, defense attorney, and some victim fragment of yourself as defendant, everybody attacking and defending until the noise in your bathroom, bedroom, car, office, mountaintop cave is deafening. No opinion is left unchallenged. No conclusion is ever reached. You're terrific at your work, but you're a terrible parent. (Sometimes the messages are mixed.) You're fat. I'm not. You're getting old, no one will love you. I'm not old, and my dog loves me. I'm strong. You're a wimp. I'm powerful, I just got a promotion. And people do love me, I've had lunch company every day for two weeks. Yeah? What have you got for Monday? I got good reviews on my last project. What you've got is lines between your nose and your mouth, no pecs, no abs, and a body the rest of which is going south. And I told you not to marry…and your father said…just as I always told you…

This is not self-awareness. This is not self-knowledge. This is self-absorption which can lead you into craziness or psychoanalysis which can easily give you understanding without any relief.

To be self-aware, to have self-knowledge, is to observe what you're hearing, doing, thinking, feeling, without judging, without calling yourself even more names. And when name-calling happens, just shift from voice-thoughts into watchful meditation to observe the name-calling without agreeing with the names. The shift into meditative listening may, as usual, first bring on a flurry of your concerns and worries, then the emptiness all those voices are trying to fill. I do a few OM's, deep-breathing, more OM's until the shift occurs.

— • —

Our own personal and self-centered emptiness yields to something more universal. The sparks of emptiness return to their source…we begin to appreciate the two-faced nature of emptiness — it fills us with dissatisfaction as it opens us to our own mystery.

Mark Epstein
Going to Pieces Without Falling Apart

— • —

What else will happen, as you sit still and allow your mind to go through the sound barrier into silence, is you will discover what bothers you, what the conflict is all about that is making your brain call you names. Then you will find clear directions about the right course to take underneath or behind the noise.

All those voices you hear inside your own head are just vocalizations of your own concerns about yourself, your life, and the ways in which you think you are being weighed, perhaps found wanting, perhaps then left by the way. It is all about psychological survival. Thought, remember, responding to the past invents the self out of its memories, experiences, knowledge, and says, "I am this, I am that, I am someone who likes this and does that, who doesn't like this and doesn't do that." At the core of our thinking is always me. The brain wants two things: security, and a sense of permanence. Neither is possible. But the self seems to supply both, so despite our discovery of its gappy, constantly fluctuating unreality, we struggle to keep its image of itself alive. We do this with our romantic attachments, or marriage, a relationship to a person, our job, religion, country, organization, church, mosque, temple, community — we seek identification to give our selves the permanency we rightly suspect doesn't exist. We simply can't bear it that there is nothing permanent, that everything changes. And so we go on insisting on having a self, an identity, whether or not it gives us pain with all its hollering, its pitfalls, whether or not it steers our course in appropriate directions.

An example: I have scolded my child for unacceptable behavior. She cried. I feel guilty. The voices in my head argue. Bad parent. Bad child. I have to teach her for her own good. At the top of your lungs? But if she does that at school, the teacher, her friends — you know the routine. It can go on forever. But when I got quiet, sat in my sitting meditation place, and let the noise die down, it was clear all I was worried about was whether my daughter still loved me or not, whether I had tarnished my image of myself as good/mother, whether it was my fault behaviorally or genetically she did what she did. It was equally clear that what was judging me was not loving intelligence but the societal memory collection in my head of family/community instructions. A moment's quiet without the name-calling made it clear it was my responsibility to teach her less mature nervous system appropriate behavior and

manners to cooperate with others, but that I did not have to ac-
quit my responsibility to my child at the top of my lungs just because I was scared of being found out a bad mother. Further, was
there a way of expressing my concern for her welfare without the
usual, human mechanical programming of turning my fear into
anger?

This, for me, was a triumph over inner thought-wars and outer
conflict with another, albeit diminutive, human being.

People these days always seem to be worrying about who they
are. Who you are is passing, and not very important: a writer, a
doctor, a union leader, a factory worker, a personal assistant, a
line-backer, a president of something.

But it's what you are that is important: kind or mean in spirit
or behavior, compassionate or self-centered. These states come in
and out like the tide. Track them. We all go through all states from
time to time.

What we are asking is, can there be an observation of the self
without the 'I' coming into it — because it is the 'I' that contains
the echo chamber for all those remembered voices of personal and
collective and biological past. And all those voices, all those perceptions are the 'I' now, are the 'you.'

It is extremely difficult to see this with the human brain. Logic
and thinking are not the enemy: but we have got so used to using
only these tools, we overuse them and forget we have the other
tool — careful and caring observation.

Each moment brings the new, the unexpected event, feeling,
reaction. We can bolt and run, or stand still and face it down. In
my experience, every time I have bolted in the face of a difficult
moment, I have only had to face it all over again. It is also interesting to discover that in each new moment there is eternity; that
now is always. And it doesn't work to greet each new moment of
eternity with a set of rusty old rules.

In quantum physics, it was discovered that the observer affected the observed and changed what it was observing. Meditation, observation, careful attention is absolutely capable of changing particle behavior — and behavior as well as everything else is changing all the time.

— • —

Neither self nor things are continuously existent...All of them resemble successively lit bulbs in the skysign or the successively explicated states we interpret as particles...it is rather hard to assert that there is...a category called 'real' which is wholly uncompromised by the observing mind.

Alex Comfort
Reality and Empathy:
Physics, Mind, and Science in the 21st Century

— • —

"Thou art that." The Sanscrit doctrine...asserts that everything you think you are and everything you think you perceive are undivided. To realize fully this lack of division is to become enlightened...Logic presumes a separation of subject from object, therefore logic is not final wisdom. The illusion of separation of subject from object is best removed by the elimination of physical activity, mental activity and emotional activity.

Robert M. Persig
Zen and the Art of
Motorcycle Maintenance

— • —

All the great minds seem to be saying: if we're not careful, all we will see is what we are already — and there's a lot more information and people and world out there than just us. Intellectual grasp of psychology, physics, metaphysics, cognitive science is extremely interesting, but it doesn't help. Just living this attentive way brings understanding.

S top reading and test this out, if you like. There must be some thing disturbing you. Most of us are constantly disturbed by something. List on paper the thoughts you generally have about a problem that is bothering you now. Then sit quietly until an entirely new attitude about the problem comes to you.

O ur brains are about three pounds of cells that coordinate our senses. There's no central 'I' anyway, as we have come to see, but there are receptor cells to receive the underlying intelligence of the universe (that some call god or consciousness), a kind of cable TV hookup to the cosmos. These receptors can know the truth about any situation because right action, right attitude isn't based on choice as if it were a mood. It is based on seeing and understanding what is right for any given situation. There is, for instance, never a right choice for cruelty, for prejudice, for killing, for ruining the environment. These are mental illnesses, illnesses of individuals and groups, caused by a breakdown of the receptors that link your life to the living universe. Obviously right action and attitude is based on what's good for everyone, not just you and yours (it is also practical, as people without what they need tend to start revolutions to get what they feel deprived of). And while we may need the technological knowledge of preceding generations so that every generation does not have to start all over again with reinventing the wheel or how to perform brain surgery, there's little point in asking them how to live life: after all, we continue to suffer, to cause suffering, and have not yet begun to run the world without suffering.

"The {brain}…is a system of organs of computation designed by natural selection to solve the problems faced by our evolutionary ancestors in their foraging way of life…[It] is designed to solve many engineering problems, and thus is packed with high-tech systems each contrived to overcome its own obstacles," says one of the leading cognitive neuroscientists Steven Pinker.

But:

— • —

The faculty with which we ponder the world has no ability to peer inside itself or our other faculties to see what makes them tick.

Steven Pinker
How The Mind Works

— • —

Jonathan Weiner the biologist rattles purely scientific paradigms or models of the origins of behavior in his book on behavioral genetics *Time, Love, Memory*. "Time, love, and memory suggest an inner world, a private realm where science can't go. At the same time, time, love, and memory refer very literally to three constellations of genes that shape our sense of time, sexual instincts, our ability to remember and forget — science's first inroads into that subjective world." He suggests genes themselves are ancestral memories of life on earth, and in that sense our ability to learn and remember is itself a memory. Science learns more and more what the brain does and what science can and cannot discover.

Some scientists think we have made progress in the four and a half million years since we first began to walk upright, and in the two million years since homo habilis, the 'handymen,' first used tools, and since the anatomically modern humans, homo sapiens, entered the cognitive niche between 200,00 and 100,000 years ago and infested the entire planet.

Other scientists think the human species has actually regressed, as our wars are still killing our own offspring, still destroying the very environment we require for life to continue.

A scientific note about so-called progress from the great science writer Stephen Jay Gould comes from his book *Full House*. He says that there is no evolution to a human pinnacle of life. He states that there is just variation in the great bush of life, lots of changing varieties of a great many species. Humans are only one variety of life, complicated but not necessarily better. After all, he repeats, 80% of life is still bacteria, not us. What we have is "consciousness — the factor that permits us, rather than bacteria or other species so far as we know, to ruminate...but how can this invention be viewed as the distillation of life's primary thrust or direction when 80% {of life} enjoys such evolutionary success and displays no trend to...complexity — and when our own neural elaboration may just as well end up destroying us." His point is that humans have arrogantly — and clearly mistakenly — appointed themselves the top dogs of creation.

Awareness, then, is to understand that this selfness we have all been educated to believe is so precious, is, in point of fact, not only a fluctuating, impermanent illusion, but the source of suffering. When those in need of logic inquire, "If there is nobody after all at home, who then is suffering?" the answer is clear. Thought creates the self, the self creates images of itself and its importance, and when an arrow hits one of the images (I am smart, powerful, right, and you tell me I am not so smart, not so strong, wrong), the image hurts. It's only image I have of myself that suffers, and being able to see this is real freedom and power.

— • —

To accept naturally without self-importance:
If you never assume importance
You never lose it

Lao Tzu
The Way of Life

— • —

The meek shall inherit the earth.

Jesus of Nazareth
New Testament, The Bible

— • —

Meek did not mean groveling: it meant those without self-importance. And when the same teacher spoke of the Eye of the Needle (an actually narrow place on a well-traveled route), what he meant by the rich man getting through with his fat camel-bags also included those with fattened heads and egos.

What the great minds of all times and cultures seem to be saying is much the same thing, and can be discovered by each of us: behaving ourselves without self-importance is freedom and the power not to suffer.

Note: We have all wondered, perhaps, why more people don't travel this country, the inner life of the mind. It's because it's hard country. Few people travel here, as there is no material profit, no promotion, no security. But for those who make the journey, the resultant beauty and joy, is worth the difficulty. Freedom is the reward, from the suffocation and pain of the life of the self. This land has a grand sweep, no certainty. Those who go there have no choice.

It must be repeated that everyone, every brain, has the capacity to travel here. Some say that only the educated, or only the genius, only scientists or philosophers can access whatever capacities lead to understanding — people like Galileo and Einstein, Christ, the Buddha, Krishnamurti.

What Galileo and Einstein, Christ, the Buddha, Krishnamurti said, though, is that thought and education and science alone are not the paths, that we can all do it, that every brain as this ability. David Bohm added, that since we only use about 15% of our brain cells that we know about, imagine what all those unconditioned cells could do. What it takes, they all said, is to be able to listen, and you can only listen in silence.

We need to be alone sometimes.

We need to sit and find silence.

CHAPTER EIGHT
Success And Failure:
Money And Other Measurements

Comparison, the constant and chronic measurement of our selves, causes a great deal of our inner anguish and outer conflict, the agonies we inflict on ourselves and the pain we cause others. There rides on every human being's shoulder that How'm-I-Doin'?-Bird to goad us on toward success and deride for failure every moment, every action, of our lives. We have been taught to measure ourselves by daily or life-long accomplishment, by money, by status and position, by physical attributes, by the opinions of others as evidenced verbally or in rewards. Comparison is the psychological killer because it makes you nervous, whether the comparison is positive or negative. If you do badly by comparison, you feel worthless; if you do well by comparison, you push yourself to stay ahead till you drop.

The trouble with comparison and measurement against not only others but some artificially marked measuring tape of our own internalized social standards, is that we all live in a state of anxiety bordering on frustration that leaves us teetering if not actually screaming on the razor edge of anger and impatience with ourselves, our families, our coworkers, and other drivers on the literal and figurative road.

It begins in childhood from the very start.

Joe is good at football, but you're as smart at math as your rich Uncle Harry.

This may sound all right on the surface, but what you're actually hearing is that you're an unmacho klutz and you'd better take the revenge of the nerds on your brother, and get rich or disappoint the entire family. Also, Joe will hate you for life because he's been informed of his own stupidity in the face of his smarter brother.

You may win the Pulitzer prize for neurobiology, Gloria, but you could learn from your sister's manners and elegance.

Gloria will kill herself trying to win the Pulitzer, but it will never make her feel all right because she will always envy the femininity and social approval of her sister and other women. So if she doesn't win lifelong competitions for prizes, she's a failure and underachiever, and if she does win, she's still a social failure and underachiever.

My kid wins more games (gets better grades, is taller, thinner, prettier, faster, makes more money, is more popular) than I ever won, got, was, ran, made at that age.

This comparison is deadly. Your life has been laid out for you from the beginning and is henceforth a long, long and endless, competition to be better than your proud parent for the rest of your years. You are special. You're better than all those other children. The worst of it is, you get out into the world and discover several other million people have been told the same thing and consider themselves far more special than you. Does that mean you're worthless after all? Were your parents lying to you to cover up the fact that you are profoundly useless? Now you have to spend your life proving or disproving this either way.

It may not be necessary to live this way any more. Millions of years ago, as hunter-gatherers, we had to compete for our very survival with other animals in forest and savannah; and the food went to the fastest, the smartest, the strongest. Any chimpanzee who didn't keep up with the troop, any gazelle who didn't keep up with the herd, any goose who didn't fly with the gaggle, got no drinks at the water hole, no forage or kill to share in, and got left to die and be eaten by predators. Today, most of us have access to the supermarket or local produce which we have invented money to buy, and it is no longer necessary to be a competitive killer to eat. Any evening news report will announce that there is plenty to go around, and if not, there is enough technology to increase everyone's share. It is no longer necessary to be a competitive killer just to stay alive.

Comparison has taken over the role of necessity, however, in turning us into competitive killers. Comparison teaches children very young that it is necessary to compete: for approval; for a place in the sun; for love and favor and more rewards than anybody needs, if not for actual food and water.

Comparison teaches us even more profoundly that we are never all right the way we are. Watch your child's face, or your friend's, or your husband's, or wife's, or employee's face when you compare them or their performances to someone else. Watch your own inner feelings, when you are compared to someone else. Even if the comparison is favorable, the mental questions begin:

If you say that about that person to me, are you making comparative statements about me to others?

Am I really better?

Do I have to try harder to stay better?

Could your opinion change with the next wind that blows?

All comparison creates is anxiousness, even anger at the presence of a yardstick, someone else's yardstick or the constant hammering of a yardstick that is used by one or another inner voice. Measurement by comparison creates internal demons that last a lifetime, whether they are grades at school, performance scores at work, lists of winners by team, project, poll. It creates tension, ambition, greed, lust for the prize, and an amiable willingness to do anything to win that may or my not stop short of grand larceny or gunshot, at least in the heart.

What we don't see, because we have accumulated so many bad habits, is that we can stretch ourselves to the fullest capacity, develop all our skills, and do our absolute best without once mentioning the words success and failure, better than, not as good as. People do not have to spend their lives, birth to death and all the moments in between, glancing sidelong at each other or in the mirror and wondering how they are coming off and what happens to them if they fail.

Listen to yourself in your sitting meditation today and note your own measurements, how often you ask yourself how you are doing, by what you measure how well or badly you are living your life. Are you enough? As in, are you accomplished enough, far enough along on your to-do-list, attractive enough, fit enough, young enough, old enough? Compared to what? In this sitting discover as you watch the flow of the outer world into your inner world, and the effects it has on you, as well as images you have told yourself or been told you have to live up to and those effects on you, what comparisons have driven you to — either into a small corner of the world where you have given up trying, or into the fierce competition for trophies that leaves you prone to heart attacks, mood swings that veer between depression from failure to the highs of a win that drive you on to the next win like an addict to the next hit.

You can easily see that you can do and be all you wish and have the capacity for. Competition is just doing something to beat others. Performing at your own best level saves all your energy to live and extend yourself to your fullest capacity.

Before you sit, you might try the following stretches to illustrate the psychological point physically.

Side Bend

Stand, legs under hips, raise your arms over your head, bend sideways from the waist, lifting the ribs up and out of the pelvis, to the left and to the right, holding the position with your head between your arms face forward, feeling the stretch in the side.

Forward Bend

Stand, legs under hips, raise your arms over your head, bend slowly forward from the hips with arms extended as a table, continue down, keeping knees straight but not locked until you are hanging from your hips, inverting upper body, and hold position, increasing the stretch to the legs if possible, relaxing entirely the torso, head, arms, face muscles, and in the relaxation feel the muscles stretch out.

Sitting Stretch

Sit on the floor, legs extended out first in front and then spread wide, keeping knees straight — raise arms overhead and bend over both legs in front, then over each leg, keeping back straight, not humped. Raise, or place pillow under knees if necessary.

Practice these stretches, without comparing yourself to another, until your body feels good, extended, relaxed.

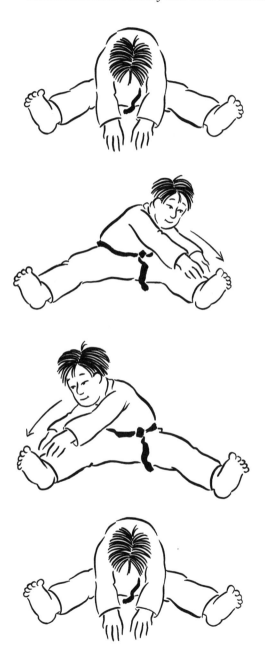

Many people talk about good and bad selves, higher and lower selves, loving one's self, self-esteem, fulfilled selves, empty selves. What seems clear is that no version of the self is healthy, and that those few who live caring, full lives are those few who manage, for a lifetime like the greatest sages, or even for a few minutes at a time, to base action on perception, on insight into what is needed, not on expanding the self.

— • —

...the human psyche finds comfort in alternately embracing...the two poles of the false self: namely, the grandiose self developed in compliance with the parents' demands and in constant need of admiration, and the empty self, alone and impoverished, alienated and insecure, aware only of the love that was never given.

Mark Epstein, M.D.
Thoughts Without A Thinker

— • —

Noting all the faces and tricks of our selves, can we move beyond them and do what is necessary for everyone including ourselves, but not based on ourselves.

CHAPTER NINE
Loneliness, Suffering,
Depression

Loneliness, suffering, depression, sadness, sorrow, grief, self-pity — these states of being are the painful discovery of our own emptiness, the feeling of being completely cut off from everyone, everything else. Much mental illness, according to contemporary brain experts, seems to be due to biochemically induced imbalances and distortions that interfere with function. (Not forgetting an abusive childhood as well as genes can cause biochemical and developmental distortions.) But even without a diagnosed mental illness, we are all aware of moments, periods, of psychological alienation. Because most of us have not been educated about how our minds and brains work, because we have not been told that the mind is normally empty, that there is no actual self, the discovery of our emptiness fills us with fear. Even people with a strong sense of self know the self comes and goes, stops and starts, has many gaps and glitches, and experience fearful moments when the self temporarily disappears.

Criticism of my work is my own personal nemesis and that of others for whom work forms the core of their identity or self. Being wrong, being found out to be wrong, is difficult for many people. Losing face, when some image of the self gets punctured or blown away, leaves people angry from the terror of sudden loss of self, of sudden emptiness. In some cases the death, divorce, the absence of another person who defined one's sense of self, on whom one was dependent for meaning, causes the grief of feeling hollowed out. Retirement, job loss, money or possessions or status gone with the wind, can make the sense of self vanish. This emptiness and fear cause depression and lead us to all the escapes that hurt us even further.

Even without the crisis of loss, we suffer, especially from our misunderstanding about nonclinical depression. There may be

depressions from an emotionally or physically distorted child-hood. There are depressions in the teen years, when you don't know if you are child or adult. There are depressions in midlife because you aren't certain where you've been or where you're going, in your work life, in your sex life, as parents of your children, as children of your aging parents. There are the griefs of growing old, of facing the eventual leaving life altogether. Something needs to be said about lumping all downer feelings under the umbrella word of depression. Not only is depression just a cover word for fear, anger, grief, it is also universally used to describe simply states of quiet, rest between activities, aimlessness as one wanders between stages of one's life. We are taught in our culture to stay high and ecstatic at all times — to ride the wave, gun the motor, fly, leap, succeed, win, be in love, live on the edge at all times or be considered 'out of it.'

Take a nap. Rest. Quiet down. Contemplate. Think. Meditate. None of these states is considered productive in a world speeded up, and any mood that lasts is unthinkable is a world divided into sound bytes. Long, lazy rainy afternoons of the soul are feared and rejected as depressions that will never end and so can never be enjoyed. An inclination toward sleepy hibernation in winter that we share with other animals is viewed with alarm. In our culture, we have been informed that we are to 'be happy,' to always 'be up,' thus inviting comparison between how we or someone else felt yesterday. And also in our culture, we are told by every commercial that happiness is 'gettable' by pursuing any of the pleasures on offer.

It is, instead, perfectly possible to look at this emptiness, to see it for what it is. Instead of seeing the empty mind, those spaces between thoughts and activities, as a beautiful, quiet, empty pool for beauty to pour into us, it scares us. Because few people talk about this as something precious and truly wonderful, we fill it

with busyness or rush into various addictions to fill the void —
other people, from our children to our lovers; accumulations of
money, possessions, alcohol, drugs, pills — and when these fail,
we use work, television, sports, clothes shopping, gambling, the
computer, movies, music, social work, books, whatever works as
escape from loneliness and depressed feelings.

The very thing loneliness wants is for something real and alive
to come in. But how can anything be poured into a full cup?
There have been times, surely, when you have taken a walk or sat
by a window in radiant sunlight when you had the extraordinary
feeling of being alone, with the whole loveliness of life and light
pouring into you. Then you already know being alone feels whole,
holy, full to the brim, in connection with everything. It isn't the
same feeling as loneliness.

Loneliness is frightening, a terrible enemy. Loneliness can create serious depressions, sufferings so bad that people drink themselves into alcoholism, drug themselves into addiction, gamble
themselves into lifelong debt or loss of their homes and families,
obsessive sexual fantasy, terminal isolation, suicide, or murder-
ously criminal rage. In women, depression usually takes the form
of suicidal isolation; in many men, the form of anger and antiso-
cial behavior. For disenfranchised people, the war-torn, the eco-
nomically deprived, for minorities deprived of personal dignity
and rights, in some cultures for women altogether, depression can
be explosive.

The fear in loneliness is that it will never end. To see that we
can be alone, empty without fear, is to understand the truth about
it. Once you see it, the panic is over. Not only will lonely feelings,
if you can stay with them, turn into the joy of being alone, but
because the world and its problems and challenges continually
present themselves, both loneliness and those wonderful moments

alone will pass. People will come into your life and go. Events will come into your life and go. The tides come in. The tides go out, and you're fine.

Just wait. They'll come in again. They always do.

All that is necessary is for the mind to understand the utter uselessness of trying to fill its own emptiness with dependencies, whether these are on knowledge or beliefs, movies or drugs, people or activities. When your mind makes friends with its emptiness, the fear goes away.

As writer, publisher, teacher, and general book nerd that I am, I am often asked as guest-person-in-residence to visit schools both in the United States and abroad. The students range in age from their teens to young adults to college and university levels, and to the fully adult teachers and professors who request workshops.

In India, I once asked a class of mixed ages and genders, students and professors alike, to describe loneliness. Their phrases were astoundingly similar to similar classes on the shoreline of Connecticut, a school in a beautiful valley in California, in New York City's Harlem. Keep in mind that a billion people live in India, usually together in large, extended families, and that there is almost no possibility, never mind vocabulary, for physical privacy, for actual physical loneliness.

As always, I began the class with group silence. I dropped the word loneliness into our silence. Twenty-three quiet teenage Indian girls and women in their salwar-kameez and saris, and twenty teenage boys and formally-dressed male teachers and professors were dutifully quiet. We did several deep breaths. The sounds of babbler birds and the whisper of the breeze through the leaves of the pipal tree stirred the dust and heat of India's long, hot afternoon. The sudden shrieking of monkeys ended our silence.

"We have been discussing the human psyche — mind as attention and perception, and brain as material, neurochemical processes of memory that produce feelings and thoughts that invent a separate self — for some time now, and we share the language of our discussions. Without invading anyone's mental privacy and with full respect for personal details, it would be helpful to all of us if anyone wanted to begin the dialogue on what you discovered about loneliness. What does loneliness feel like to you?" I asked.

An Indian male student in his mid-teens answered:

"For me, loneliness is the feeling of being completely cut off from your family –there is nothing you can depend on." In India, family is everything and everyone.

A woman teacher raised a shy hand from the folds of her sari.

"Loneliness is like dying all the time. You can't feel actually the touch of anything or even any person. You are in the dark, by yourself, you cannot communicate, even with the husband who lies next to you, even with your children. Everything, everyone is far away."

A teenage boy in a Connecticut class wrote:

"What loneliness feels like is a deep, sunless pain, as if you had been flung into a dark corner of the universe, or beneath the depths of the sea. No one can reach you."

A Harlem graduate student said:

"Even when you get it that the self isn't real, it still feels real, and it — you — still feel lonely."

Men and women, boy and girl, Indian and American, all said the same things. In every country and culture, we all seemed to feel the same feelings and have the same thoughts about the suffering and depression of feelings of loneliness even if we understood intellectually that isolation was literally only an intellectual position.

In the classroom in India, there followed a discussion of the physical and intellectual evolution of hominids over our four-and-a-half million years into the sole surviving hominid of which all of today's populations are members: Homo sapiens. What was obvious to the group was that while biological and intellectual evolution was complex, and the faculty of human thinking had produced technology, politics, economics, education, religion, and the varieties of science such as neurobioolgy, psychology, cognitive neuroscience, evolutionary anthropology, our evolution as a species, while it had developed the intellect, had left other human faculties totally undeveloped. We still acted like ground squirrels defending their holes — only now we had vicious weapons. Why couldn't we see this and change? Why could we not see that invention of a separate 'me' that is terrified of not being important enough to survive is at the basis of our violence – and stop muscularizing it.

— • —

We are all, to some degree, chemically imbalanced. It is not only the addict, the diabetic, the paranoid schizophrenic, the chronic depressive whose brain and glands suffer from disabilities. Anyone who has had an unhappy childhood, abused with wrongful ideas, prejudices, preconceptions, evangelical myths, carries mental disabilities not necessarily evident to the naked eye. A rotten childhood changes the chemistry as well hypoglycemia, and as long as we operate from the mythical self, and defend it, the chemical changes brought on by this activity alter sanity in each one of us. It isn't only those who carry Ouzis and lead out the tanks, those who drop bombs and hunt small, helpless animals and call it sport who propagate violence. It is all of us because we all possess and defend ego.

And then, instead of watching self as it arises in the moment and defusing it, living attending to it, we look for a savior and, as in the Jonestown massacre, we become KoolAid drinkers....

Ray Fisher
Unpublished Works

— • —

I have a friend who often says, in fewer words than this book,

— • —

If this occasion is not my wedding, I may not be the bride.

Joanne Cozzolino
Special Education Teacher

— • —

Over and over, we are all saying the same things: I am lonely; loneliness is awful; but I can't seem even to want to give up its cause — ME!

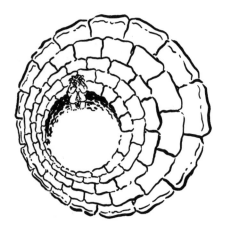

Instead of giving up the separate 'me,' what we all do is search frantically for an escape from the loneliness and the suffering it causes, some kind of rope to pull us up and out of the deep well of loneliness, or some manner of boat or raft to sail out of the empty seas to shore, or at least across the river to any bank but our own. We go on hoping that some one, some practice, some method, can do for us some kind of magic trick so we can keep our selves and still not suffer.

— • —

It is a rare being who can cross the ocean of existence without a boat.

Richard Alpert (Ram Dass)
Journey of Awakening

— • —

Psychotherapists, teachers, friends, lovers, organizations, methods — we use all of these as boats, just something to carry us for a while until we can get our balance, our strength back, to continue our journey.

The trouble with using boats, though, is they can turn into traps and prisons, and weaken you into illusions of safety that, like desert mirages of a pleasant watering hole under drifting palms, only delay your journey toward freedom from pain.

Boat rides, rest stops, hideouts under magic safety quilts, the whole trade in safety craft are perceptive distortions we all invest in sometimes. But if you do use a boat from time to time, think of it as a temporary raft, not a safe haven. Don't confuse it with the real thing. Don't confuse being in love with loving; good works with goodness; a sermon about god with your own real connection to god. My own downfall is often confusing good works with goodness; I can get on a very high horse because I am a rehabilitator of small wildlife, I teach children, I write and publish mental health and meditation books; and I experience a sense of well-being from being such a good girl. All of this does not necessarily shorten my temper or lower my arrogance. There is still a well-defended 'me' that still needs constant attending.

Pondering the following insights can help:

- To know we are all, we hominids, in the same psychological situation, that all human beings think all the time, all feel very similar desires and fears, and so, in the pit of loneliness, you can hold hands with the rest of us lonely souls.

- Meditation, awareness, is the awakening of intelligence that sees there is no 'me' and no 'you,' no 'we' and no 'they,' and that only a small part of the brain involved with thought has created all this separation (remembering that meditative attention in daily life is not self-improvement, it is the ending of the self and its problems).

- So if 'I' and 'you' are dissolved, even for a few moments, separation ends and therefore loneliness ends (happens often enough at the height of love-making, which is one reason the human race likes love-making).

- It helps to remember that you can use a different part of your brain than thought as the disssolvement of the self (awareness, insight, universal receptors, those receivers every brain has for the intelligence of the universe to come through).

- Attention will show you that loneliness is often just a habit of thought, like anger, fear, and so many other psychological aches and pains — feelings we have read about, been taught to feel when we are alone, rather than something we actually feel.

- Experiment leads to the discovery that being on your own, being alone, is not the same as loneliness: it can be like climbing a mountain — hard going at first, but in the end, exhilarating and freeing.

Sometimes nothing helps in passages of loneliness. You have to just sit it out until it passes and you can use your intelligence to see through loneliness once more.

As you can tell from this book, when I get stuck in some deep, dark place inside myself, I use writing meditation. I just write about what's going on with me until the bits of self dissolve like stains in clear water. And when the specks won't dissolve, when I get too stuck in my own psychological and spiritual melodrama, I also remember the prayer of St. Francis when he went through his own emotional troubles.

Lord, make me a channel of thy peace…grant that I may seek rather to comfort than be comforted, to understand, than to be understood, to love, than to be loved. For it is by self-forgetting that one finds.

People find it helps to engage in dialogue, to share with others experiencing the same feelings. You can try a two-to-five minute group silent sitting and have a dialogue afterward about relationship, and loneliness.

People also find that it ends loneliness to share in cooperative community activity. It is said a civilization is judged by how it cares for its least members, its most helpless populations. These days, the whole planet is at stake, entire ecological systems, people, animals, plants, the very air we breathe. We must understand the biological, scientific, not just sentimental, truth that without animals and plants there will quite simply be no us. Not only because human beings cannot thrive alone, but because it coarsens us not to care.

— • —

Our relationship with each other suffers from our relationship with everything else, animate and inanimate. Is it any wonder that human beings are so irresponsible in their actions to one another, when they are equally dismissive of animals and the natural environment?

Alan Kishbaugh, president of
California conservation federation;
executive director of
Krishnamurti Foundation America

— • —

In the West there is loneliness, which I call the leprosy of the West. In many ways it is worse than our poor in Calcutta.

Mother Teresa
Missionaries of Charity

— • —

CHAPTER TEN
Education And Money

— • —

People pay very little attention to how they are thinking. They don't see that all these crises are due to the way we think. They say they want to solve these crises, yet they want to go on with the same way of thinking. It doesn't make sense.

David Bohm, Theoretical Physicist
Dialogue with Students
Oak Grove School, CA

— • —

Professor P. Krishna, an eloquent, international educator, once remarked to a gathered throng of people, "Surely the urgency of change in the way we have been conditioned and educated, and continue to condition and educate our children, strikes any alert adult." By alert, it was clear the speaker meant anyone engaged in the act of breathing.

There was another teacher who announced to her class that she thought grades were as dangerous to people's minds as an armored tank was to their bodies, that they would not be given grades by her, that they would only be given a pass or fail based on the completion of their work. She watched their original enthusiasm fade into disappointed dismay.

An interesting inquiry probably most searchingly explored by keeping the question on a back burner throughout a twenty-four period instead of a brief sitting is: what were the primary purposes or values of my education that I am passing on now to my children, either by example or in the educational system my taxes pay for?

Surely the fundamental purpose of education is not to reproduce robots, cultural soldiers to propagate and defend to the point of war and their own deaths whatever they consider their personal or local systems. Surely the purpose of education is to develop human beings to their fullest capacities of intelligence rather than pain and suffering, and encourage freedom rather than cause the regimental authority that forces everyone to goose-step to the same beat.

Of course education must provide knowledge and the skills necessary to earn our daily bread.

Of course education must uncover individual talents and capabilities in each student.

The above, most schools are good at. It's the third 'of course' in which we fail.

And of course, education must awaken in each human being an understanding of the myth of separation in each psyche and the even deeper understanding of every human being's connection and therefore global responsibility to everyone and everything else, to the wholeness of life, not just a few convenient fragments.

Javier Gomez Rodriguez, international teacher and writer, suggests that the following educational aims inform all schools, as well as the teaching of the necessary skills for jobs, careers, professions:

1. *Skill in action: the way one speaks, eats, walks, studies, behaves.*

2. *A close relationship with nature, not to destroy the things of the earth.*

3. *A view of humanity as a whole: each of us is the world.*

4. *A deep sensitivity to beauty which is more than the appreciation of art.*

5. *A quality of affection and care for all things, of love and compassion.*

6. *The awakening of intelligence or insight beyond mere intellectual capacity.*

Javier Gomez Rodriguez
On Education
The Link, No.16, 1999

Knowledge of the self and our habits of thinking is essential in any education because one of our habits is not to listen directly but to interpret everything we hear according to our prejudices, likes, dislikes, whether we are a Russian, a Jew, Muslim, Hindu, Rastaferian, Abenaki, communist, American, Italian, rich, poor, whatever group, caste or class we belong to. To truly learn, we must be able to see these positions, and see through them, in order to see at all.

To go back to the classroom where the teacher announced the withdrawal of the grade system — what is wrong with our educational system that our students only want to learn in exchange for grades, and what does that teach us about living our lives subsequently? What would make places of education different so people actually want an education? After all, what the survival of our species is based on and one of the factors that distinguishes the human brain, is curiosity: about the stars and the workings of the universe; about ourselves, the purpose of our lives, our place in the whole spectrum of life in the cosmos; about nature, about the nature of life itself.

Why, and at what point, did this natural interest in learning warp out of shape and turn into fear in the form of a scramble for success that in school takes the form of good grades and thereafter a killing race for money and power?

It is we, the adults, who must see that education at school as well as at home is an expression of our intent in shaping the world, and our responsibility — and we must see that it is the neglect of the psyche in our education and in our teaching of the next generation that brings on the world's calamities.

In your own exercise in examining the purposes of education, see if you agree with your conditioning. See what attitudes about cooperation and competition you've been handed down, what has changed in your lifetime, what you would like to hand down to the next generation yourself. What are your reactions to the following comments from students in a Midwestern high school class?

"My family expects good grades. They expect me to learn to measure up, not just in science and math and English, but in sports, in popularity, everything."

"I want my father to be proud of me, not think of me as a failure."

"I can only get into a good college or get a good job if my marks are good."

"What's the point in doing the work if you don't get good grades?"

"I'm scared to go home if I don't get good grades."

These students, like so many others, expose the hypocrisy of our educational system. We have taught them to keep an eye on the prize, on the piece of paper at the end, the one without which we won't give them a degree, without which we won't give them a higher education, a decent job, money to live on, a place in society, respect. After all, we have created a society in which there is no room for an honest poor man, an intelligent poor teacher, an old woman in household service. Without grades, a lot of students would probably not do the work, flunk themselves out, and go get jobs they don't like. This actually might be a good thing!

Young people might end by hating the boring, repetitive jobs, come back and really want to learn something meaningful, apply themselves to engineering to replace factory work, or hotel management to replace fast food service, or developmental psychology to augment domesticity. They might discover they want to learn carpentry, masonry, engine repair, how to run a small business. They would come back to school motivated to learn so their lives might be stimulating and fulfilling instead of boring, meaningless. And they might insist on an excellent education because they were paying for it, because they knew the penalty of living out ignorant, repetitive days, day after boring day.

It's no good telling each other and our children that after all we have to compete to survive: in fact, we don't. Particularly in countries like the United States and India, there are plenty of land and water resources to feed everyone with plenty left over to export, either in sharing or in trade. This fierce competition is a power game, nothing more.

Even as young as preschool, society begins to teach its children to compete, to envy, to battle each other for preference or for the best grades. We use the excuse that we have to teach them skills to make a living. Of course we do all have to learn those skills in math, science, writing, and so forth so we can make a living. But if we don't also teach skills in relationship, in the art of living, we don't end up with a cooperative, productive society. We end up with combat.

The same children who hit each other over the head with shovels in the sandbox, the same children who competed for grades, the same children who were not taught the beauty of a flower but only its name to repeat on a test, will turn into adults who trample life instead of loving its bloom.

The blooming of human beings, that's what education is for, to help them use their energy in living creative, not destructive, lives; to help them discover what interests them, not us; to discover their own talents, to make a living at or at least to enjoy occupying themselves with in their spare time.

— • —

In our stress and struggle with our children to get their skills accomplished, there is the opportunity for us to examine ourselves as parents, as people, as grown up children. After all, we want more for our children than for them to join the rat race of competitive career chasing and ladder climbing. There appears to be more conflict in the world, in our communities, and in our schools than ever before. What is it our children are really learning? What are they observing and attending in our lessons and the classes at school?...We, as parents and early childhood caregivers are responsible for examining in ourselves what we think we are teaching and what our children are learning.

Hannah Carlson, M.Ed., C.R.C.

Living With Disabilities

— • —

The real issue is the quality of our mind: not its knowledge but the depth of the mind that meets knowledge. Mind is infinite, is the nature of the universe which has its own order, has its own immense energy. It is everlastingly free. The brain, as it is now, is the slave of knowledge...Education then is freedom from conditioning, from its vast accumulated knowledge as tradition. This does not deny the academic disciplines which have their own proper place in life.

J. Krishnamurti, October 1,1982

Letters to the Schools, Vol. 2

— • —

— • —

Change your thinking now. If you don't change your thinking now, tomorrow will be the same as today.

Ray Fisher
Unpublished Dialogues

— • —

The odds against your being able to blow away an educational system like candles on a birthday cake are as formidable as the transformation, the mutation, of even your own single brain. With the odds so great against saving our lives, against saving life on our planet, why keep on trying to save anything at all?

The real question is, how can we not keep on trying! What each of us can do is examine our own motives in educating ourselves and our children, pay attention to our own attitudes, and lay new paths in our own brains with different behavior, different thinking that produces cooperation; not separation. Just changing an attitude affects not only the chemistry in your own brain, but everything else, whether the change is immediately visible or not. When speaking about these educational matters to others, stand your ground. How often have you heard something that made no sense to you at the time but that you understood days, weeks, years later on? So, plant seeds.

You can share with your children the understanding that mere rebellion is a waste of time and energy. It is revolution that counts, and revolution is an inside job. If you speak differently, whether at home at the dinner table, at school meetings, in community dialogue, if you change your own attitudes about education and what it means, you can change other attitudes wherever you go. Personally, I mutter without letup.

As always, begin with yourself, your own family, your own children. If you just see the truth of something, it will change your life, because you won't be able to buy into the lie anymore. Then you can talk to receptive teachers at schools, colleges, universities, in community groups. Don't be concerned if you sound different. As we all know, a million people can be absolutely wrong.

Money is something else, like sex, we have made a problem of. There's nothing either meritorious or bad about money. It is what it is, a simple form of trade agreement, a trading commodity, easier to carry in your pocket if you want to buy a truck than a flock of chickens to trade. And if you don't have any money, then someone else has to house, feed, and clothe you. People resent doing this for healthy people over the age of eighteen. Also, if you don't have any money, you can't give any money away to help anybody else. But money is simply what it is, no less and no more. Only neurotics and people with too much of it look down on money with contempt. Only lunatics think money defines a man's or a woman's worth. Only frightened and greedy people think money is personal power, status, influence. Any intelligent person has surely noticed that the most powerful, influential status in history has always come from that rarest of all things, not money, but goodness. Whose names have lasted longer than Jesus Christ, Mohammed, Buddha, Mother Mary, Mother Nature, God?

We've been talking about the brain's conditioning: in different countries, different qualities are valued and taught to the young. The qualities may be equally spurious, equally arbitrary, but they disprove that economics are invariably the basis for respect. In China and Japan, duty, to family, country, corporation, is the measure of a person. In France, intellect and lineage are the measures of their aristocracies and neither can be bought. In India, despite legislation, caste. In England, class. In the United States, meritocracy is based on winning evidenced by money and celebrity.

When I traveled and taught in India, I watched and eavesdropped as I roamed villages and cities. What struck me was the shocked muttering of Americans looking at India with Western eyes instead of through Eastern lenses, clucking over what they called India's poverty. Particularly in Mother Teresa's Calcutta, where so many of us worked with the Missionaries of Charity in the Mission for the Destitute Dying, Americans stared at families living on a patch of pavement with their children and their few pots on a bit of cloth, bathing publicly at the street pump and sharing with affection for one another what little they had like the poor from Appalachia to the South Bronx or anywhere else. What the Americans could not see was the ugliness in their own faces, the poverty Mother Teresa saw in their loneliness, and their paranoia, the fear that what they had might be stolen from them.

Money, we tell our children, is the reward of the ambitious. Our culture has taught that without ambition, nothing is accomplished: good grades, leading to good colleges, leading to good jobs, leading to better jobs and more money. But is it true that without ambition, nothing is accomplished? A carpenter can build a beautiful house without ambition, because he loves to build and it is how he earns his living. A machinist can become an electrical engineer because she wants to build an extraordinary car, not because she wants to be president of General Motors and earn a lot of position and money. Perhaps far more can be accomplished for the love of it, whatever the work we do, than for financial reward. Of course, we must be paid: we have outlawed slavery in any of its manifestations. But during rush hour, look at all those tired, miserable faces in traffic jams, or when you're shopping in malls, watch people plugging away at work they find boring, repetitive, mechanical, for their whole lives, because they've been taught to live with ambition for more position, for more money, and then to spend it on things they don't need. An interesting and terrifying fallout is the situation of both parents working twelve-hour days so they can live in upscale neighborhoods with upscale possessions to send their psychologically orphaned children to upscale schools. Is there a point?

An interesting meditation: What have you given up for money or status in your life?

Unfortunately, in the last few thousand years (and we've been around for millions, so the history of money is pretty recent), money has assumed disproportionate symbolism. It has become, because of our educational system both at school and at home, an interpretive value in and of itself. Ambition, after all, is just one of the manifestations of self-importance that any reflective mind can see is a trap, another bar on the prison of the self. It is no longer based, as we have seen, on physical survival in this century but a lingering vestigial item like the bump on the end of our spines that was once a tail. Can we break with habit and tradition and the jail of ourselves so that our children can live and enjoy what they do instead of being shackled to the runaway machinery of accumulation?

What we must not do is misunderstand the values of education and money. Clearly, both are useful, both are fun. But there is little point to confusing function with position, function with status or power. For one thing, there's always going to be somebody who has more position, more money, more power. Success is only another of society's inventions to control people, especially its young. True value may not include external measure.

— • —

Let go the things in which you are in doubt for the things in which there is no doubt.

Mohammed
The Koran

— • —

CHAPTER ELEVEN
Love

Our music and art, our novels, movies, our soap operas and real operas, the most secret as well as overt fantasies of our culture, all seem to be obsessed with a neurotic disturbance. It is that compound of sex, biology, loneliness, the need for security, the passion for possession and power, dependency in a relabeled need for parenting, and addiction with its desperate highs and equally desperate withdrawals, an inability to stand on one's own two feet, the emptiness that requires drama and a part under spotlights in the eternal movie script — all of which we have called 'being in love.'

People who are determined not to mess up their lives, people with a scrap of intelligence, see through an addiction to romantic attachments in people who defend being in love all the time as simply an attempt to rationalize chemistry. Intelligence distinguishes between speaking English (or Arabic, Japanese, Cherokee, Swahili) and speaking lovetalk. From country music lyrics to grand opera, being in love is described in phrases generally used to describe a panic attack when you're experiencing paroxysmal tachycardia.

How can we promise to 'love forever?' You will or you won't. It's one day at a time like everything else. Marriage vows, in any case, were invented when people only lived two or three decades. A dozen years was not much of a forever to expect compared to the six, seven, even eight decades of today's romantic forever.

Nor are we especially fussy about love. We say, I love you. Equally we say, I love pizza. I love god. I love that movie. I love my mom. I love my country. I love football, blue jeans, the hot tub. What are we going on about?

When we say, aren't I supposed to love my race, my nation, my group, what are we talking about? Not only has technology connected the world too closely for parochial distinctions, but we are biologically global as well. We are human beings, not labels, and, like cats, all belong to the same species. We have artificially created nations and races in our search for power over each other and some illusion of security; and through greed, ill-will, and general idiocy out of which we arrange for prejudice, war, drive-by shootings, slavery, and holocausts. What's so hot about loving all this? Only madness has resulted in our impossible pursuit of an unchanging security that exists only in children's dreams.

And when we talk about a love relationship, what we really mean is the security of ownership.

An interesting experiment to try the next time you have a quiet moment with friends is to ask them what they mean by 'love.' My own friend, the philosopher Ray Fisher, once asked me that question some years ago, and the way I answered made me sound as if the person I said I adored was a country I was conquering. Ask your friends, or just listen to them when they talk of loving, a lover, or mate, or child. What you'll hear is, "he's mine," "she's my girl," "that's my wife," "my husband says." Think how often, as you gaze adoringly at a mate or a child across a room during parenthood, a love affair, or marriage, you've heard or said or thought, "you belong to me."

Marriage, if it is a good marriage, is a place where you can learn the truth about yourself and grow up, mature, where there is freedom, generosity, affection, the sharing of the chores and joys of life; above all, there is good will. Too often, there is a part of us that wants the security people find in prison, not only physically but in the daily familiarity of easy, repetitive feelings — bitterness, self-pity, and other negative feelings so easy to feel. This makes what after all is supposed to be a mutually beneficial contract, the contract from hell.

— • —

The humorless rigidity of the traditional Western attitudes to love and sex have made the prison exceptionally grim and the security astonishingly impregnable. The grimness of the prison has been most evident in the kind of emotional blackmail which couples have inflicted upon one another ...in the pretense that love between two people who have met when fairly young, and have usually married for unconscious reasons with a strong neurotic content, can supply all that is needed, emotionally, intellectually, sexually — for growth over what may be a period of fifty or sixty years...

Forms of slavery in marriage are not far to seek. The husband bitterly bound to the responsibilities of making money, the wife determinedly sacrificing her gifts and talents...bound by guilt, by what their parents thought about marriage...As slaves do, they take their pain out on one another, playing deathly games in which selfishness, anger, and hate are dressed up to look like unselfishness, patience, and love...We can only set ourselves free from such sickness by going deeply enough into ourselves to find the courage to see what we are...[then] it will be possible for our marriage partners, or anyone else, to relate properly to us.

Monica Furlong
Ordinary Magic: Everyday Life
As Spiritual Path

— • —

The slavery implied by ownership is not love. Clearly, love is not jealousy either, or possessiveness, pride, security, dependency, a drug-of-choice, a hiding-place from the confusion and loneliness of life. It is not just a word to be used about parents, child, mates, friends, pets, rituals, because of all the gratification they give you. Love is not the activity of do-gooders and politicians, ambition or acquisition, either. 'I just love Alabama' generally means 'please vote for me.' 'I love my art collection' is almost certainly self-congratulatory. And 'I love the poor' out of anyone's mouth but the Missionaries of Charity unclothes the poor of their single possession, their resilient dignity.

— • —

Love is not to be divided as the love of God and the love of man, nor is it to be measured as the love of one and of the many. Love gives itself abundantly as a flower gives its perfume; but we are always measuring love in our relationship and thereby destroying it...

In the total development of the human being through right education, the quality of love must be nourished and sustained from the very beginning...this quality of love, which is humility, gentleness, consideration, patience, and courtesy. Modesty and courtesy are innate in the person of right education...considerate to all, including the animals and plants, and this is reflected in behavior and manner of talking...[It] frees the mind from its absorption in its ambition, greed.

J. Krishnamurti
Total Freedom

— • —

Love is the ultimate and real need in every human being.

Erich Fromm
The Art of Loving

— • —

Obviously. Ask anyone. So none of this means don't be in love with your sweetheart, don't love the rocky hills and the winter silent snows, the teeming streets and the sacred places of the country you live in, the generosity of your parents and teachers, the sport or music you love to play. It simply means don't use them for your own gratification (dependency and need and control are taking, love only gives), and don't exclude everything and everyone else from that affection. It means don't have images for someone to have to live up to, no rules, no regulations. This does not mean we are free to be promiscuous or to be inconsiderate; it means don't keep a suit of shining armor or a size six string bikini in your garage that someone has to fit into or be found wanting. These images we make up, these fantasies, prevent connection with anyone psychologically. We relate to pictures our thought makes up of people, and we live in isolated dissatisfaction, bitter disappointment, and loneliness when people don't match the movie we have made up about them.

Love is a state of being. It is not attached only to one person or object. Where the self is, with its uproars of thoughts, needs, dependencies, expectations, and images, love is not.

All we need, really, is a shift in our perception, our understanding about love. If it isn't global as well as personal, what we are feeling is certainly something, but it probably isn't love.

Certainly, you have suspected all this. Certainly, you have heard the words, I love you, and known perfectly well:

1. The person facing you wasn't capable of love.

2. The person facing you was only capable of loving her or his own self.

3. There was the smell of mendacity in the air, betrayal, a bargain-hunter with a neon sign that read 'you do this for me, I'll do that for you.'

But never mind other people; there is not much you can do about them. What you can do, is be mindful of yourself and change your own ways of acting and relating.

Take time to sit quietly by yourself. You might like to try something called vipasana.

Vipasana

Vipasana is a focus on the breath. A courageous woman, a prison official named Kiran Bedi, arranged for thousands of prisoners in India to learn vipasana. Teachers were sent to the prisons and asked to help these violent and miserable human beings go on an inward journey, to see if watching and understanding their own minds, their own ways, lessened the incidents of their violent behavior. It was an interesting journey for many of them. They sat still, without speaking, focusing on the breath only, so that the mind did not wander, for ten days. Some reported that after three days, they were able to have a physical sensation without immediately reacting to it; anything from a powerful urge to murder someone to an itch from a mosquito bite. No one pretended that vipasana was a lifetime cure. But by delaying one urge at a time, those who took part in the vipasana meditations committed fewer violent words and actions in their daily lives.

Ten minutes to begin with, in vipasana, will do.

Do a few stretches first, a martial arts or yoga or aerobics or dance exercise to release the body's muscles, two or three OM's or AMEN's in the most comfortable of your lower voice tones. Make sure these tones resonate in your head. You might light a candle for company, incense for soothing nerves. Outdoors, sit under a tree, near water, on a park bench. Watch the light for a moment.

Sit, if you are home, as usual, on the floor with legs crossed, both feet or one foot resting on the opposite knee, or, not to cut off circulation, one leg bent at the knee in front of the other. There are several forms of lotus position possible as long as the spine is erect, the body and head centered. You can sit on a chair, in your usual sitting place, legs down, feet firmly planted. Close your eyes. Breathe slowly, deeply, naturally, in and out. Simply follow the breath with your attention. Focus on inhaling and exhaling, nothing else. You will feel your breath softly above your lips after a while. Feel nothing else but the air going in, coming out.

Your mind will wander off, into this or that thought, along this or that fantasy, plan, through the list of things you must do, what people have said to you or you to people. Don't yank or scold. Just bring your focus gently back to the breath every time it wanders. In and out. In and out. Mind your back so you don't lean or slump. Keep it straight so the lungs are free to breathe properly.

You will begin to make some discoveries. That it is your own reactions to the outside world and people that create your actions, not the world itself. Watch your emotions, pain, pleasure, come and go. You will see nothing stays permanently with you, none of these feelings lasts. Hatred, passion, greed, envy, joy, affection, ecstasy, unwillingness to let go, resistance to change, and all their physical sensations come and go. Let them and their physical sensations pass without reaction. Just observe, as in, there's anger, there's anxiety, there's pleasure, there's love.

This silent focus on the breath is a marvelous opportunity to examine the inner country of one's own consciousness and its contents, its passions, its opinions, its urgencies, and one's mind.

The prisoners said this kind of meditation, this kind of observation, changed them from mean and miserable beings into people who can stand themselves. We might pay attention to their experiment, all of us being prisoners behind our own bars one way or another.

— • —

The development of our own cerebral cortex has resulted in the thrills of intellectual achievement...but can you imagine when the probe creatures from another civilization arrive how they'll react with horror at the mindless, hideous, primitive creatures they encounter here?

Fox Mulder,
alias Chris Carter
X-Files

— • —

CHAPTER TWELVE
Truth, God, And Death

Truth, god, and death are all the same in a way, if you ponder it. The truth is, as we've discovered, that the self, with its predilection for living according to blindly obeyed tradition perhaps once based on survival necessities but no longer necessary, repeating like a mechanical robot over and over whatever it has been told — this self and its actions is the problem. And when we hang on to the content of our consciousness and at the same time try to go beyond it, the conflict kills us.

All our racket, prayer, and ambition, really all the same thing, gets in the way of our connection to the universe and the joy of living; it is not our pathway to it. Silence alone is the place where connection is possible, whether between one human and another, or between us, the birds that fly, and the sky. And truth. And god.

You have discovered for yourself in silent meditation, that the death of the self, even its absence for a few moments at a time, leaves only intelligence, truth, connection, love, goodness; in another word — life.

The body does not have to die for you, that is, your self with all the content of your consciousness, to die.

Every time you have done a sitting as you've been reading this book, or when you have taken a walk alone, or done a task without thinking of your self and its problems, or even when you have been listening to the voices of your suffering in a detached, impersonal way, or really listened to another human being or to beautiful music, or really seen and touched a tree, or smiled good morning to a stranger, or picked up trash somewhere unasked, or taught someone younger a life skill — whenever you have looked at the world or anyone in it with new eyes instead of old ideas — in those moments, your self has died and something else, whether you call that God or Love or the Spirit of the Universe, is there.

However hard we try to fix it, mold it, better it, love it, criticize it, refurbish it, rename it, the self (and all its little selfs) is trouble. It is lonely, cut off, feels separate, no matter how many cars in the garage, no matter how much money, prestige, or shoes it owns. And it also doesn't matter how many boards of directors it sits on, groups and teams it belongs to, how many friends it has, raises it gets, how cool its lover, how big its family, how industrialized and powerful its tribe, nation, religion. In the very act of making itself grand, it makes itself separate, lonelier than ever.

But here we are, stuck with the self that the human brain, all human brains, invent. Just seeing this to be the truth makes our stuckness easier. At least we won't invest the self with more importance now than it already feels.

When Jesus said, "Die to be born again," he knew what he was talking about. He may not have meant the death of the body that comes before entering heaven, but the death of the self. You don't have to actually wait until you die to reincarnate, as the Eastern religions suggest. You can die and reincarnate into a better and happier place this afternoon. You can see on your own the truth that the death of the self leaves place for Life, God, the Universe to pour in, and that truth, god, and death are one.

As for physical death, the death of the body, what is it but a return of atoms to atoms? We've only coined the word 'death' for this return and our own sense of loss. Everything is made of the same stuff in our universe, we and the trees and the stars. We, it all, came out of the same material, some physicists say a big bang, when all the matter in the universe exploded out of a single density. Says Stephen Hawking, a cosmological physicist, and one of the great minds of the twentieth century, "There was a time, about ten or twenty thousand million years go, called the big bang, when the universe was infinitesimally and infinitely dense. Everything came from the exploding matter of that density, that ball of matter."

— • —

One may say that time had a beginning at the big bang, in the sense that earlier times simply would not be defined...One can imagine that God created the universe at literally any time in the past...the universe is expanding [objects like stars and galaxies, once close together, are observably flying apart from each other in the universe around us like spots on a balloon blowing up] and there may be physical reasons why there had to be a beginning...An expanding universe does not preclude a creator, but it does place limits on when he might have carried out his job!

Stephen W. Hawking
A Brief History of Time from
the Big Bang to Black Holes

— • —

All creative minds, physicists, metaphysicists, thinkers of all kinds, respect the mystery of the universe, whatever name they give it. Something not us created matter out of nothing at all, and we still do not even understand the Principle of Life. The human brain did not create a tree, or itself, for that matter, and that's that. Call whoever or whatever did create it all anything you like.

And also, among our other thoughts, thought has invented the idea of death. As we've said, there really isn't such a thing, only the physical change we call death. When my five-year-old grandson Chaney asked me about death one day, I explained to him that since we are all made of stardust (and we are!) we simply turn back into stardust again (we do!) Whereupon, he picked up his shirt and stared down at his little belly in awe. I could see in his eyes, that he was looking into his belly at the stars. He was still too young to separate himself out from everything else with the thought-invention called a self.

So, once again, we are stuck on the business of the self. Some call it a soul, an atman, a godhead, the Buddha or the Christ in us. But what is it we want to go on living forever? This suffering self? This boring, frightened, petty, needy, little bundle of nerves?

Why not let it die now. And never fear death again.

Therefore, what we discover is that nothing stays the same, everything changes. This is encouraging if you are feeling bad, and you are delighted to know it will pass. But if you like things the way they are, you don't want to anything to move. Of course, even if you like the way things are, the human brain gets bored easily, so even sweet moments turn sour if they go on long enough. How long can you make sex last, even with someone you're mad about, without getting hungry, wanting to yawn, or change the subject to sports, business, shopping, or the kids? You may like to run marathons or climb Everest, but even runners and climbers have, at some point, to stop or drop. On the cheerful side, the ending of one thing is the exact moment the next thing begins, even if your shutter speed is too slow to catch the new image for a while.

My favorite illustration that the great truth is, nothing ever dies, came from a science fiction movie, the original version of *The Incredible Shrinking Man*. In the movie, the hero was exposed to radiation while he was out in his boat. At home, as a result of the exposure, he began to shrink, bit by bit, until his clothes, his house, his life became too large for him. Eventually, his cat chased him down into the cellar, where he nearly drowned in a few drops of water. He made his escape out onto the lawn, where even the mown grass was a jungle. He stared up at the universe, and remembered his science. It doesn't matter how infinitesimally small I get, he remembered: nothing in this universe disappears.

Nothing disappears, nothing is lost, joy is as available as the next breath.

Sit down. Get silent. Let go of the burden of yourself. And breathe free.

— • —

Come, come, whoever you are,
Wanderer, worshipper, lover of leaving — it doesn't matter.
Ours is not a caravan of despair.
Come, even if you have broken your vow a hundred times
Come, come again, come.

Jalal-ud-din Rumi
Persian Sufi Mesnevi Poems

— • —

Suggested Reading And
Selective Bibliography

Most of the people and works that are fundamental to understanding the nature of meditation (that is, paying attention to the nature of the self in daily life) have been mentioned in the text and quoted in the quotes: the *Bible,* Old and New Testaments; the *Koran;* the *Vedanta,* the *Gita,* translated by Christopher Isherwood, 1972; Lao Tzu's *The Way of Life* (Tao) translated by Witter Bynner, 1998; the Penguin 1973 edition of Buddha's teachings, the *Dhammapada; Zen Mind, Beginner's Mind,* Shunryu Suzuki, 1979. Those mentioned below and all the works of J. Krishnamurti are especially relevant to meditation in daily life, as he speaks in particularly accessible twentieth-century language, and even more particularly as he has influenced some of the greatest scientific as well as psychological/philosophical/spiritual minds of this century.

You will want to read a wide variety of meditation writings from African cultures, both East and West Indian cultures, Peruvian, Chinese, Japanese, Persian, Tibetan traditions, the early Christian saints, the Muslim and Jewish scholars, and books by scientists like Albert Einstein, Stephen Hawking, David Bohm, Alex Comfort whose work constantly suggests the connection of the human brain with the physical universe. Many of these writings, as well as work by scientists in the fields of neurobiology, psychology, sociology, anthropology have also informed this book. An accessible science writer is Stephen Jay Gould; an accessible psychotherapist is Mark Epstein. Major sources for facts and statistics in this book were newspapers, journals, magazines, especially *U.S. News and World Report*, government publications, almanacs, public television specials, documentaries, news broadcasts, and particulalrly Ted Koppel's *Nightline*.

Many of the books listed have already been mentioned in the text of this book.

Carlson, Dale and Hannah Carlson, M.Ed., C.R.C. *Where's Your Head? Psychology for Teenagers*. Madison, CT: Bick Publishing House, 1998. A general introduction for adults and young adults to the structure of personality formation, the mind, feelings, behaviors, biological and cultural agenda, and how to transform conditioning in our education systems.

Comfort, Alex, M.D., D.Sc. *Reality and Empathy: Physics, Mind, and Science in the 21st Century*. Albany, State University of New York Press, 1984. An overview of the physics, metaphysics, and philosophy of science.

Dass, Ram (Richard Alpert). *Journey of Awakening: A Meditator's Guidebook.* Revised. Edition. New York: Bantam Books, 1990. This American psychologist is also a spiritual teacher who has studied and practiced meditation in its many paths of mantra, prayer, singing, visualization, and 'just sitting,' to movement meditations like tai chi — and suggests various paths to find a personal, suitable invitation into meditation for each person.

Dennett, Daniel C. *Counsciousness Explained.* Boston: Little, Brown and Co., 1991.

Epstein, Mark. *Going to Pieces Without Falling Apart.* New York: Broadway Books, 1998. A psychiatrist's discovery that Western psychology's emphasis on the strengthening of the self and the ego is deeply flawed, that meditation as well as psychotherapy brings the understanding of letting go of the self and its inherent self-centered suffering. Also *Thoughts Without a Thinker.* New York: Harper Collins, 1995.

Goldstein, Joseph, and Jack Kornfield. *Seeking the Heart of Wisdom: The Path of Insight Meditation.* Boston: Shambala, 1987. The many forms of meditation lead to quieting the brain so that insight can take place.

Gould, Stephen Jay, Ph.D. *The Mismeasure of Man.* New York: W. W. Norton, 1996. Dr. Gould's challenge to the hereditary IQ as a measure of intelligence and destiny. Also *Full House.* New York: Three Rivers Press, 1996.

Hittleman, Richard. *Yoga: 28 Day Exercise Plan: 500 Step-by-Step Photographs.* New York: Bantam Books, 1980. Simple exercises, step-by-step instructions, photographs teach yogic secrets of breathing, concentration, muscle control, relaxation, resulting in relief from pain, freedom from stress, more energy, more focus.

J. Krishnamurti. *Meeting Life: Writings and Talks on Finding Your Path without Retreating from Society.* San Francisco: Harper Collins, 1991. Perceptions and wisdom on love, society, death, self-censorship, relationships, solitude, meditation, fear, anger, relationship to society. *The Book of Life: Daily Meditations.* Edited by R. E. Mark Lee. Harper San Francisco, 1995. Day-by-day, month-by-month insights into our passions, concerns, problems, freedom, and transformation. *Krishnamurti: Reflections on the Self.* Edited by Raymond Martin. Chicago: Open Court Publishing Company, 1997. *Total Freedom.* Harper San Francisco, 1996. An excellent introduction to the essential Krishnamurti.

Merton, Thomas. *New Seeds of Contemplation.* New York: New Directions, 1961. An exploration of the inner journey emphasizing that what we need, what we seek, is inside us all the time.

Persig, Robert M. *Zen and the Art of Motorcycle Maintenance: An Inquiry Into Values.* New York: Bantam Books, 1981. Father's quest for himself and right values as he takes his son on a journey across the country by motorcycle, and examines the relationship of technology, science, and our educational systems to true quality in living life. *Lila: An Inquiry into Morals.* New York: Bantam Books, 1991. A sailboat carries the philosopher and a mysterious woman named Lila on the same kind of voyage of adventure and ideas.

Trungpa, Chogyam. *Meditation in Action*. Boston: Shambala, 1996. This Tibetan meditation master and Western teacher explores the ability to see clearly into situations and deal with them skillfully, going beyond formal practice into creative living without the self-consciousness of the ego. A brief manual, and to the point. Also see Trungpa's *The Myth of Freedom and the Way of Meditation*. Boston: Shambala, 1998.

Van Clief, Ron. *Manual of the Martial Arts: An Introduction to the Combined Techniques of Karate, Kung-Fu, Tae Kwon Do, and Aiki Jitsu for Everyone*. New York: Rawson Wade Publishers, Inc., 1981. Step-by-step, movement-by-movement postures in this manual show you how to move through this self-instructional course in various of the martial arts. Basic and advanced.

Welwood, John, Ph.D. *Ordinary Magic: Everyday Life as Spiritual Path*. Boston: Shambala, 1992. Thirty-five essays by well-known spiritual teachers, therapists, writers, artists reveal how the simple practice of mindfulness can transform anyone's daily life.

Directory Of Meditation Centers, Retreats, Teaching Groups

The following is a list of national centers that teach practices of quieting body and brain so that meditation in daily life is easier. Proper physical exercise, proper breathing, healthful eating, the integration of personal and social living, mindful attention to the self, nature, the universe, the connection of everything to everything, right living, these are teachings in many centers, foundations, institutes that follow. For local groups near you, call these national centers, ask your local church, temple, mosque groups, your exercise, yoga teachers, look in your telephone book.

BRAHMA KUMARIS WORLD SPIRITUAL ORGANIZATION
Church Center for the United Nations
777 United Nations Plaza
New York, NY 10017
(718) 565-5133

The Brahma Kumaris World Spiritual University now has nearly 2,000 branches in over 50 countries, and serves as a nongovernmental organization of the United Nations. It offers retreats, conferences, workshops, individual and group classes at all levels of spiritual practice. Meditation and counseling therapy are available for adults, young adults, and special groups: AIDS patients; the physically disabled; drug and alcohol dependent.

HIMALAYAN INSTITUTE
RR 1, Box 400
Honesdale, PA 18431
(717) 253-5551 — (800) 444-5772

Yoga and meditation for personal growth of the individual and for the sake of society, for better health, for self-awareness to attend to various aspects of mind, body, emotions, mental balance. Stress management, biofeedback, natural health care, workshops, retreats, meditation, yoga programs.

INTEGRAL YOGA INSTITUTE
227 West 13th St.
New York, NY 10011
(212) 929-0585

Yoga, breathing, relaxation, concentration, meditation, chanting, self-inquiry for every aspect of the individual: physical, emotional, social, intellectual, and spiritual. There are 27 national teaching centers, and yoga homes connected with the institutes at many branches.

KRISHNAMURTI FOUNDATION OF AMERICA
Box 1560
Ojai, CA 93024
(805) 646-2726

The world influence of the nonsectarian religious teachings and meditations of J. Krishnamurti is carried on by the work, the schools, the publications, of the international Krishnamurti Foundations in California, India, England. There are contacts and study groups all over Europe, the Far East, Latin America, Australia, Hawaii, Russia, Africa. Associated with the foundations are schools, study centers, retreat groups for the young as well as adults. These were established for those who want to understand life and themselves, and how to live a meditative life in the world without running away or dropping out. Call, for books, schools, literature, membership to receive Bulletins.

SELF-REALIZATION FELLOWSHIP
3880 San Rafael Avenue
Los Angeles, CA 90065
(213) 225-2471

Unites East and West in an understanding of the fundamental harmony of all religious paths, with temples, retreats, meditation centers around the world. Network of groups and individuals serving those in need, worldwide prayer circle, homestudy series of yoga and meditation, spiritual and humanitarian work. Write or call for free literature and further information.

THE THEOSOPHICAL SOCIETY IN AMERICA
PO Box 270
Wheaton, IL 60187
(312) 668-1571

This is a nonsectarian body of seekers after truth, a Brotherhood of Humanity, to study comparative religion, philosophy, and science, to practice and study meditation. There are more than one hundred and fifty branches, study centers, and camps in the United States.

TWIN CITIES VIPASSANA COOPERATIVE
1911 South 6th Street
Minneapolis, MN 55424
(612) 332-2436

Meditation without dogma, ritual, or cultural trappings. Clear, continuous observation of different aspects of the mind-body process. With this observation come insights into connectedness.

LOCAL CENTERS, GROUPS, RETREATS, CAMPS, WORKSHOPS

Zen Centers, Prayer Centers, Shambala Training in Tibetan Buddhism, Moslem Groups, Christian Church Groups, Jewish Temple Groups, Hindu Vedanta Training, Native American Groups, Yoga Schools and Centers, all kinds of Meditation Centers and Study Groups can be found locally for your area by checking your Yellow Pages, as well as by writing or calling the listings in this book. There are camps, retreats, renewal centers, monasteries and convents, in all major and many smaller cities, associated with most temples, churches, and in many communities associated with local groups and schools. Do call first. Do ask for literature to make certain there are need-appropriate groups.

Index

Author

Dale Carlson
Author of over fifty books, adult and juvenile, fiction and nonfiction, Carlson has received three ALA Notable Book Awards, and the Christopher Award. She writes novels and psychology books for young adults, and general adult nonfiction. Among her titles are *The Mountain of Truth* (ALA Notable Book), *Where's Your Head?* (Christopher Award), *Girls Are Equal Too* (ALA Notable Book), *Stop the Pain: Teen Meditations, Wildlife Care for Birds and Mammals. Stop the Pain: Adult Meditations* follows her teen meditation book. Carlson has lived and taught in the Far East: India, Indonesia, China, Japan. She teaches writing and literature here and abroad during part of each year.

Illustrator

Carol Nicklaus
Known as a character illustrator, her work has been featured in *The New York Times, Publishers Weekly, Good Housekeeping*, and *Mademoiselle*. To date she has done 150 books for Random House, Golden Press, Atheneum, Dutton, Scholastic, and more. She has won awards from ALA, the Christophers, and The American Institute of Graphic Arts.